KÖNEMANN

© 2019 koenemann.com GmbH
www.koenemann.com

ÉDITIONS
PLACE DES
VICTOIRES

© Éditions Place des Victoires
6, rue du Mail – 75002 Paris
www.victoires.com

ISBN : 978-2-8099-1671-3
Dépôt légal : 2ᵉ trimestre 2019

Editorial project: © Loft Publications S.L.
loft@loftpublications.com

Editorial coordinator: Claudia Martínez Alonso
Assistant to editorial coordination: Ana Marques
Edition and texts: Marta Serrats
Art director: Mireia Casanovas Soley
Translations: textcase

ISBN: 978-3-7419-2377-7 (international)

Printed in China by Shenzhen Hua Xin Colour-printing & Platemaking Co., Ltd

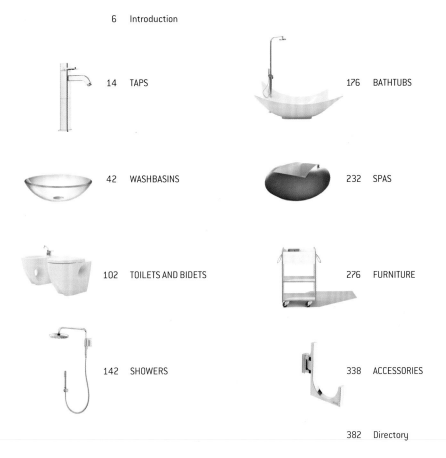

6   Introduction

14   TAPS

176   BATHTUBS

42   WASHBASINS

232   SPAS

102   TOILETS AND BIDETS

276   FURNITURE

142   SHOWERS

338   ACCESSORIES

382   Directory

In recent years, the bathroom has undergone a substantial change while encompassing the use of conceptual architecture, design, elegance and functionality. The health culture and the cult of the body—not to mention the proliferation of spas—have spurred many designers in their attempt to incorporate these principles into the home. Even though bathrooms are still primarily functional, they are often viewed as more than that and are no longer merely deemed as a space where we engage in our daily grooming routines.

Some cultures, such as in Scandinavia, Japan and the Arab world, have been privy to this knowledge for centuries. In those countries, the bathroom is a significant place inside the house and receives as much attention to detail as any other room. Large bathrooms are a must and are used for stretches at a time to relax and recapture a sense of wellbeing. Essential oils and the texture of natural stone associated with Japanese baths or the candles and fresh flowers used in the Arab baths make these bathrooms a pleasure for the senses.

As these trends gradually reached the rest of the developed world, interior designers and architects began to rethink the aesthetics of the bathroom. Exceptional examples are a bath and mirror set designed by Jaime Hayón for the Spanish company Artquitect, and oval-shaped bathtubs designed by Ross Lovegrove for Vitra.

Of course, technology has played a major role in this shift. Home shower massages, jacuzzis, saunas and other water therapy devices have become affordable to many people.

Nowadays there is an infinite variety of materials suitable for bathrooms. Marble is still a prominent choice, especially in elegant bathrooms, and even though glass and stone have gained ground it's hard to imagine that they will ever become more stylish than ceramic bathtubs. Wood elicits warmth, and varieties like teak are preferable since they are more durable. Small glass mosaic tiles add colour and texture and can be used either to cover an entire area (floor and wall) or as an ornate detail (such as the outside of the bathtub). Metal and plastic resin are water-resistant and are increasingly used in the design of modern bathrooms. Even water-resistant paint, when properly applied, can bring a touch of colour, as long as the bathroom is well-ventilated.

Despite the wide range of trends these days, minimalism is still in the vanguard. Minimalist bathrooms follow the principle of "less is more", especially with regard to light and space. One of the most common choices is white ceramic bathroom fixtures with use of glass, marble and chrome steel in the accessories and other elements. The lines are neat and streamlined. Towels and other bathroom items are stored in built-in cabinets and drawers so that nothing obscures the bathroom's symmetry and viewing angle.

The exact opposite trend in bathroom design, maximalism, has also increased in popularity. Maximalist spaces are imposing with bright colours, metallic finishes and sinuous, rounded shapes. They are often inspired by 18th and 19th century interiors. Maximalism leaves room for a more eclectic, personalised style.

Of course, there is a gamut of variations between these two extremes. You must simply explore the boundaries of the bathroom space, know your budget and, most important of all, let your imagination soar in order to turn your bathroom into your own sanctuary of respite.

Au cours des dernières années, les salles de bains ont fait l'objet d'un changement important combinant concepts architecturaux, design, élégance et fonctionnalité. Avec l'émergence de la culture de la santé et du culte du corps, ainsi que la multiplication des spas, de nombreux designers cherchent à appliquer ces principes à l'environnement domestique. Bien que les salles de bains restent essentiellement fonctionnelles, le lieu transcende désormais sa fonction initiale et ne se limite plus à un espace où l'on vient faire sa toilette quotidienne.

Dans les cultures scandinave, japonaise et arabe par exemple, cela fait des siècles qu'il en est ainsi. Dans ces pays, la salle de bains a une place de premier plan dans l'habitat et reçoit la même attention que tout autre espace domestique. Elle continue d'occuper un grand espace où l'on se prélasse pour se détendre et retrouver une sensation de bien-être. Tous les sens sont stimulés, que ce soit avec des huiles essentielles et l'utilisation de la pierre naturelle dans les salles de bains japonaises, ou par le biais de bougies et de fleurs fraîches dans les salles de bains arabes.

À mesure que ces tendances ont été adoptées dans le reste des pays développés, les designers et architectes d'intérieur ont commencé à repenser l'esthétique des salles de bains. Nous en trouvons un bon exemple dans les designs de salles de bains et de miroirs de Jaime Hayón pour l'entreprise espagnole Artquitect, ou encore avec les baignoires ovales de Ross Lovegrove pour Vitra.

La technologie a, bien entendu, joué un rôle clé. Les douches hydromassantes, les jacuzzis, les saunas et autres systèmes de thérapie par l'eau sont aujourd'hui beaucoup plus abordables.

À l'heure actuelle, il existe une variété infinie de matériaux pour la salle de bains. Le marbre continue de régner en maître, surtout dans les salles de bains élégantes, et même si le verre et la pierre sont de plus en plus utilisés, il est difficile d'imaginer qu'ils puissent un jour supplanter l'élégance de la céramique. Le bois apporte une dimension chaleureuse, bien qu'il reste faille privilégier des essences comme le teck, qui sont plus résistantes à l'eau. Les petits carreaux de mosaïque de verre ajoutent une touche de couleur et apportent une texture. Ils peuvent être utilisés pour recouvrir des surfaces entières (revêtement des sols et des murs) ou comme simple détail (par exemple, pour tapisser l'extérieur d'une baignoire). Les métaux et les résines plastiques résistent à l'eau et sont de plus en plus utilisés dans le design de salles de bains modernes. À cela s'ajoutent les peintures résistantes à l'eau qui, appliquées comme il se doit, sont un moyen d'apporter de la couleur, la condition première étant que la salle de bains dispose d'une bonne ventilation.

En dépit de la diversité des tendances actuelles, le minimalisme est toujours d'avant-garde. Les salles de bains minimalistes suivent le principe du *less is more*, surtout en matière de lumière et d'espace. La préférence va en général aux meubles en céramique blanche, en verre, et en marbre et à l'acier chromé pour les accessoires et autres éléments. Les lignes sont simples et épurées. Les serviettes et autres articles de bain sont rangés dans des armoires encastrées et des tiroirs, afin que rien n'obstrue la vue et n'interfère avec la symétrie de la pièce.

À cette tendance s'oppose le maximalisme, aujourd'hui très populaire dans le design des salles de bains. Les espaces maximalistes multiplient les couleurs vives, les finitions métalliques, ainsi que les formes sinueuses et arrondies. Ils s'inspirent souvent des intérieurs des XVIIIe et XIXe siècles. Le maximalisme permet un style plus éclectique et personnalisé.

Entre ces deux extrêmes, il existe de nombreuses variations. Vous devez simplement explorer les limites de l'espace dont vous disposez, déterminer ce que vous voulez en faire et surtout, vous laisser guider par votre imagination afin que votre salle de bains devienne un lieu de détente bien à vous.

In den letzten Jahren haben sich die Badezimmer in den Bereichen architektonisches Konzept, Design, Eleganz und Funktionalität stark verändert. Die Gesundheitskultur und der Körperkult sowie die Verbreitung der Spas haben dazu geführt, dass viele Designer versuchen, diese Prinzipien in den häuslichen Bereich zu übertragen. Dadurch sind die Badezimmer heute weit mehr als funktionale Räume für den täglichen Gebrauch.

In Kulturen wie zum Beispiel der skandinavischen, der japanischen und der arabischen weiß man das schon seit Jahrhunderten. In diesen Ländern sind Badezimmer im häuslichen Bereich sehr wichtig. Die großen Bäder sind immer präsent und dienen in erweiterter Form der Entspannung und dem Wohlbefinden. Es werden alle Sinne angesprochen, sei es durch ätherische Öle, natürliche Steine in den japanischen Bädern oder durch Kerzen und frischen Blumen in arabischen Bädern.

In dem Maße, wie sich diese Tendenzen im Rest der entwickelten Welt durchgesetzt haben, haben die Innendesigner und Architekten die Ästhetik des Sanitärbereichs umgestaltet. Sichtbar wird dies in den Designs der Bäder und Spiegel von Jaime Hayón für die spanische Firma Artquitect, oder in den ovalen Badezimmern designt von Ross Lovegrove für Vitra.

Die technischen Geräte spielen dabei natürlich auch eine große Rolle und sind immer gefragter, ob Massageduschen, Whirlpools oder Saunas.

Heute besteht ein Bad aus vielen Materialien. Es überwiegt immer noch der Marmor, besonders in den eleganten Badezimmern, und obwohl auch Glas und Stein zum Einsatz kommen, werden sie die Eleganz von Keramik wohl nie in den Schatten stellen. Holz schafft Wärme, wobei Varianten wie das wasserresistente Teakholz besonders gut sind. Die kleinen Mosaikfliesen aus Glas geben Farbe und Struktur und man kann damit ganze Wände und Böden versehen oder auch nur kleine Details wie den Außenrand von Badewannen. Metalle und Plastikharze sind wasserresistent und kommen immer häufiger in modernen Bädern zum Einsatz. Ebenso können gut positionierte, wasserresistente Bilder als Farbtupfer dienen, solange die Belüftung stimmt.

Trotz all der Vielseitigkeit aktueller Tendenzen bleibt der Minimalismus durchaus modern. „Weniger ist mehr" lautet das Prinzip, vor allem in Bezug auf Licht und Raum. Besonders beliebtes Zubehör sind Möbel aus weißer Keramik, Glas, Marmor und verchromtem Stahl. Die Linien sind sauber und schnörkellos. Handtücher und andere Badartikel werden in Einbauschränken und Kisten aufbewahrt, so dass nichts den Blickwinkel und die Symmetrie des Badezimmers stört.

Genau die gegensätzliche Tendenz ist der Maximalismus, der sich ebenfalls stark im Design der Badezimmer durchgesetzt hat. Solche Räume haben kräftige Farben, ein metallisches Flair und sind gebogen oder rund. Häufig werden Sie durch die Innenräume des 18. Und 19. Jahrhunderts inspiriert. Der Maximalismus erlaubt einen eklektischen und persönlichen Stil.

Natürlich gibt es zwischen diesen beiden Extremen viele Varianten. Es müssen nur die Grenzen des Raums erschlossen werden, der beansprucht wird. Man muss wissen, was man ausgeben möchte und das Wichtigste ist: Man muss seine Vorstellungskraft wirken lassen, damit das Bad zu seinem eigenen, persönlichen Rückzugsort wird.

De afgelopen jaren heeft het ontwerpen van badkamers een essentiële verandering doorgemaakt. Er zijn vanuit de architectuur veel ideeën doorgedrongen over design, elegantie en functionaliteit. De designers proberen in het ontwerpen van onze badkamers thuis de ontwikkelingen door te voeren die gaande zijn op het gebied van gezondheid en lichaamsverzorging, ontwikkelingen die we ook terugzien binnen de groeiende hoeveelheid thermen en kuuroorden. De meeste badkamers zijn weliswaar nog steeds vooral functioneel, maar steeds vaker worden badkamers meer dan alleen een ruimte waar de dagelijkse lichaamsverzorging plaatsvindt.

In sommige culturen, zoals de Scandinavische, Japanse en Arabische cultuur, weten ze het al eeuwenlang. In die landen is de badkamer een van de belangrijkste vertrekken van het huis en krijgen de details zeker net zoveel aandacht als die in andere kamers. De badkamers zijn groot en vormen een belangrijke ruimte om te ontspannen en op adem te komen. Alle zintuigen komen aan bod door middel van het gebruik van essentiële oliën, natuursteen (Japanse badkamer) of kaarsen en bloemen (Arabische badkamer).

Naarmate deze trends hun intrede deden in de westerse wereld, zijn designers meer gaan nadenken over de esthetiek van sanitaire ruimtes. Een goed voorbeeld daarvan zijn de badkamerontwerpen en spiegels van Jaime Hayón voor de Spaanse firma Artquitect en de ovale badkuipen die zijn ontworpen door Ross Lovegrove voor Vitra.

Natuurlijk hebben ook technologische ontwikkelingen een belangrijke rol gespeeld. Zo is het tegenwoordig voor velen mogelijk om thuis een massagedouche, jacuzzi, sauna of andere therapeutische watervoorziening te laten installeren.

Vandaag de dag kan er bij het ontwerpen van een badkamer ook gekozen worden uit een oneindige hoeveelheid materialen. Marmer is nog steeds de belangrijkste, vooral in chique badkamers, en hoewel glas en steen bezig zijn aan een opmars lijkt het moeilijk voor te stellen dat deze materialen de voorkeur gaan krijgen boven het elegante keramiek. Hout geeft warmte aan het ontwerp, het liefst worden houtsoorten als teak gebruikt omdat die waterbestendig zijn. Mozaïeken van glazen tegeltjes geven een ontwerp kleur en structuur. Daar kan de hele ruimte (zowel de vloer als de muren) of alleen een detail (bijvoorbeeld de buitenkant van de badkuip) mee worden bekleed. Zowel metaal als kunsthars zijn waterbestendig en worden steeds vaker gebruikt in het ontwerpen van moderne badkamers. Daarnaast kan ook het gebruik van waterbestendige verf kleur brengen, mits het correct is aangebracht en de badkamer goed wordt geventileerd.

Er zijn tegenwoordig heel wat verschillende trends, maar minimalisme is nog altijd een van de belangrijkste hoofdrolspelers. Voor het ontwerp van minimalistische badkamers wordt uitgegaan van het principe 'minder is meer', vooral daar waar het gaat om licht en ruimte. Meestal wordt voor het meubilair gekozen voor wit keramiek en voor accessoires en andere elementen voor glas, marmer en verchroomd staal. Het lijnenspel is strak en zonder opsmuk. Handdoeken en andere badartikelen worden opgeborgen in inbouwkasten en kisten, zodat niets het perspectief en de symmetrie van de badkamer verstoort.

Daartegenover staat het maximalisme dat als trend inmiddels ook is opgekomen binnen het badkamerdesign. Maximalistische ruimtes zijn overweldigend met veel levendige kleuren, metalen afwerkingen en kronkelige en ronde vormen. Meestal zijn ze geïnspireerd op interieurs uit de achttiende en negentiende eeuw. Met een maximalistische vormgeving is het mogelijk een meer eclectische en persoonlijke stijl te creëren.

Tussen deze twee extremen ligt natuurlijk nog een groot palet aan variaties. Eenvoudigweg te bereiken door de grenzen van de beschikbare ruimte te verkennen, uit te gaan van het beschikbare budget en — wat het allerbelangrijkste is — de fantasie de vrije loop te laten, zodat de badkamer echt een persoonlijke plek is waarin je je met plezier kunt terugtrekken.

En los últimos años, los baños han experimentado un cambio sustancial que integra conceptos arquitectónicos, diseño, elegancia y funcionalidad. La cultura de la salud y el culto al cuerpo y la proliferación de *spas* han hecho que muchos diseñadores intenten transferir estos principios al ámbito doméstico. Aunque su uso sigue siendo básicamente funcional, el baño va más allá y deja de ser un mero espacio para llevar a cabo el aseo diario.

Algunas culturas, como la escandinava, la japonesa o la árabe, lo saben desde hace siglos. En estos países, el baño pasa a un primer plano de la casa y recibe la misma atención al detalle que cualquier otro espacio doméstico. Los baños grandes están siempre presentes y se utilizan de forma prolongada para relajarse y recuperar la sensación de bienestar. Todos los sentidos son atendidos, ya sea con los aceites esenciales, con la textura de la piedra natural en los baños japoneses o con las velas y las flores frescas utilizadas en los baños árabes.

A medida que estas tendencias se introducían en el resto del mundo desarrollado, los diseñadores de interiores y arquitectos comenzaron a repensar la estética del sanitario. Un buen ejemplo lo tenemos con los diseños de baños y espejos de Jaime Hayón para la firma española Artquitect o con las bañeras ovaladas diseñadas por Ross Lovegrove para Vitra.

La tecnología, por supuesto, también ha tenido un papel muy importante en el cambio que han experimentado los baños. Duchas de masaje, *jacuzzis*, saunas y otros dispositivos de terapia del agua están ahora al alcance de muchos.

Actualmente, existe una infinita variedad de materiales para el baño. El mármol todavía ostenta su dominio, especialmente en cuartos de baño elegantes y, aunque el vidrio y la piedra han hecho avances, es difícil imaginar que alguna vez superen la elegancia de las bañeras de cerámica. La madera aporta calidez, aunque son preferibles variedades como la teca, que son más resistentes al agua. Los pequeños azulejos de mosaico de vidrio añaden color y textura y se pueden utilizar para cubrir un espacio entero (revestimiento de suelo y paredes) o un simple detalle (por ejemplo, el exterior de una bañera). Los metales y las resinas plásticas son resistentes al agua y se utilizan cada vez más en el diseño del cuarto de baño moderno. Incluso las pinturas resistentes al agua, cuando se aplican correctamente, pueden proporcionar un punto de color, siempre y cuando el baño tenga una ventilación adecuada.

A pesar de la diversidad de tendencias actuales, el minimalismo se encuentra todavía en la vanguardia. Los baños minimalistas siguen el principio «menos es más», sobre todo en lo que se refiere a luz y espacio. Una de las elecciones habituales son los muebles de cerámica blanca, de vidrio, mármol y de acero cromado para los accesorios y otros elementos. Las líneas son limpias y sin adornos. Las toallas y otros artículos de baño se guardan en armarios empotrados y cajones, de modo que nada pueda interferir con el ángulo de visión y la simetría del cuarto de baño.

Justo la tendencia contraria, el maximalismo, también se ha introducido con fuerza en el diseño del baño. Los espacios maximalistas son imponentes, con colores vivos, acabados metálicos y formas sinuosas y redondeadas. A menudo se inspiran en los interiores de los siglos XVIII y XIX. El maximalismo permite un estilo más ecléctico y personalizado.

Por supuesto, entre estos dos polos existe un gran número de variaciones. Simplemente debes explorar los límites del espacio a ocupar, conocer tu presupuesto y, lo más importante, dejar volar la imaginación para conseguir que el baño se convierta en tu retiro personal.

Nel corso degli ultimi anni, i bagni hanno attraversato una fase di cambiamento sostanziale che combina concetti architettonici, design, eleganza e funzionalità. La cultura della salute, il culto del corpo e il proliferare delle spa, hanno fatto sì che molti progettisti abbiano cercato di trasferire questi principi all'ambito domestico. Sebbene il suo utilizzo continui ad essere essenzialmente funzionale, il bagno oltrepassa questo confine e smette di essere un semplice spazio per l'igiene quotidiana.

Alcune culture come quella scandinava, giapponese o araba, ne sono consapevoli da secoli: in questi Paesi il bagno occupa un posto di primo piano all'interno della casa e riceve la stessa attenzione al dettaglio di qualsiasi altro spazio domestico. I bagni grandi sono sempre presenti e vengono utilizzati molto spesso per rilassarsi e recuperare la sensazione di benessere. Tutti i sensi sono soddisfatti con oli essenziali, attraverso la porosità della pietra naturale nei bagni giapponesi, o con candele e fiori freschi nei bagni arabi.

Man mano che queste tendenze si sono introdotte nelle restanti parti del mondo sviluppato, i designer d'interni e gli architetti hanno cominciato a riconsiderare l'estetica dei sanitari. Un buon esempio lo possiamo trovare nei disegni di bagni e specchi di Jaime Hayón, per la marca spagnola Artquitect, o nelle vasche da bagno ovali disegnate da Ross Lovegrove per Vitra.

Anche la tecnologia ha ricoperto un ruolo molto importante: docce a idromassaggio, Jacuzzi, saune e altri dispositivi di terapia ad utilizzo d'acqua, sono oggi alla portata di un gran numero di persone.

Attualmente siamo di fronte ad una varietà infinita di materiali per il bagno: il marmo detiene tuttora il primato, soprattutto nelle sale da bagno eleganti, e, nonostante il vetro e la pietra abbiano fatto dei passi avanti, è difficile riuscire a immaginare che un giorno superino l'eleganza delle vasche da bagno in ceramica. Il legno conferisce calore, e se ne preferiscono alcune varietà come il tek, che risultano più resistenti all'acqua. Le piccole piastrelle a mosaico di vetro aggiungono colore e trama e possono essere utilizzate per coprire un intero spazio (come rivestimento di pavimento e pareti) o un semplice dettaglio (per esempio, la parte esterna di una vasca da bagno).

I metalli e le resine plastiche sono resistenti all'acqua e si utilizzano sempre più nella progettazione di sale da bagno moderne. Anche le vernici resistenti all'acqua, se applicate correttamente, possono conferire un punto di colore, ma sono applicabili solo nel caso in cui il bagno abbia una ventilazione adeguata.

Nonostante la differenza di tendenze attuali, il minimalismo fa ancora parte dell'avanguardia. I bagni minimalisti seguono il principio per il quale «meno è più», soprattutto per quanto riguarda la luce e lo spazio. Una delle scelte consuete sono i mobili di ceramica bianca, vetro e marmo e l'acciaio cromato per gli accessori e gli altri elementi. Le linee sono pulite e senza ornamenti superflui. Gli asciugamani e gli altri articoli da bagno sono custoditi in armadi a muro e cassetti, in modo che nulla possa interferire con l'angolo di visuale e la simmetria della sala da bagno.

Anche la tendenza contraria però, il massimalismo, si è introdotta con forza nel design del bagno: gli spazi massimalisti sono imponenti, con colori vivaci, finiture metalliche e forme sinuose e arrotondate. Spesso si ispirano agli interni del XVIII e XIX secolo. Il massimalismo consente uno stile più eclettico e personalizzato.

Chiaramente, tra questi due estremi esistono un gran numero di stili. Dovete semplicemente esplorare i limiti dello spazio da occupare, sapere qual è il vostro budget e, più importante, lasciare libero sfogo alla vostra immaginazione per far sì che il bagno diventi il vostro luogo di ritiro personale.

Nos últimos anos, as casas de banho experimentaram uma alteração substancial que integra conceitos arquitetónicos, desenho, elegância e funcionalidade. A cultura da saúde e do culto do corpo, e a proliferação de spas, fizeram com que muitos designers tentassem transferir esses princípios para o âmbito doméstico. Embora a sua utilização continue a ser basicamente funcional, a casa de banho transcende tudo isso e deixa de ser um mero espaço onde efetuar a higiene diária.

Algumas culturas, como a escandinava, a japonesa ou a árabe, sabem isso há séculos. Nestes países, a casa de banho ocupa um ponto importante da casa e recebe a mesma atenção aos detalhes que qualquer outro espaço doméstico. As casas de banho grandes estão sempre presentes e utilizam-se de forma prolongada para relaxar e recuperar a sensação de bem-estar. Todos os sentidos são cuidados, quer seja com óleos essenciais, com a textura da pedra natural nas casas de banho japonesas ou com as velas e as flores frescas utilizadas nas casas de banho árabes.

À medida que estas tendências foram sendo introduzidas no resto do mundo desenvolvido, os designers de interiores e arquitetos começaram a repensar a estética das instalações sanitárias. Encontramos um bom exemplo nos desenhos de casas de banho e espelhos de Jaime Hayón, para a empresa espanhola Artquitect, ou nas banheiras ovaladas desenhadas por Ross Lovegrove para a Vitra.

A tecnologia, claro, também desempenhou um papel muito importante. Duches de massagem doméstica, jacuzzis, saunas e outros dispositivos de terapia com água estão agora ao alcance de muitos.

Atualmente, existe uma infinita variedade de materiais para casa de banho. O mármore, todavia, tem o domínio, especialmente em quartos de banho elegantes, e, embora o vidro e a pedra tenham conseguido avanços, é difícil imaginar que alguma vez superem a elegância das banheiras de cerâmica. A madeira proporciona conforto, embora sejam preferíveis variedades como a teca, já que são mais resistentes à água. Os pequenos azulejos de mosaico de vidro acrescentam cor e textura e podem utilizar-se para cobrir um espaço inteiro (revestimento do solo e paredes) ou um simples detalhe (por exemplo, o exterior de uma banheira). Os metais e as resinas plásticas são resistentes à água e utilizam-se cada vez mais na conceção de quartos de banho modernos. Inclusive as pinturas resistentes à água, quando aplicadas corretamente, podem proporcionar um ponto de cor, sempre e quando a casa de banho tenha uma ventilação adequada.

Apesar da diversidade de tendências atuais, o minimalismo encontra-se, todavia, na vanguarda. As casas de banhominimalistas seguem o princípio «menos é mais», sobretudo no que se refere à luz e ao espaço. Uma das escolhas habituais são os móveis de cerâmica branca, de vidro, de mármore e de aço cromado para os acessórios e outros elementos. As linhas são limpas e sem adornos. As toalhas e outros artigos de banho guardam-se em armários embutidos e gavetas, de modo que nada possa interferir com o ângulo de visão e a simetria do quarto de banho.

A tendência precisamente contrária, o maximalismo, introduziu-se também em força na conceção das casas de banho. Os espaços maximalistas são imponentes, com cores vivas, acabamentos metálicos e formas sinuosas e arredondadas. Frequentemente, inspiram-se nos interiores dos séculos XVIII e XIX. O maximalismo permite um estilo mais eclético e personalizado.

Claro que, entre estes dois extremos, existe um grande número de variações. Você deve simplesmente explorar os limites do espaço a ocupar, saber qual é o seu orçamento e – o mais importante – deixar voar a imaginação para conseguir que a casa de banho se converta no seu lugar de retiro pessoal.

Under de senaste åren har badrummen genomgått en avsevärd förändring i arkitektur, design, elegans och funktionalitet. Hälsokulturen och omtanken om kroppen har tillsammans med den växande mängden spainrättningar gjort att många formgivare börjat överföra samma principer till hemmen. Även om användningen i grunden förblir densamma, har badrummen utvecklats till något mer än bara en plats där man sköter din dagliga hygien.

I vissa kulturer, som de skandinaviska, japanska och arabiska, har man varit medveten om detta i århundraden. I de länderna har badrummet en central plats i hemmet och får samma uppmärksamhet och detaljrikedom som alla de andra rummen. Det finns alltid stora badrum och de används i stor utsträckning för avslappning och välbefinnande. Alla sinnen tillfredsställs, antingen med doftoljor eller natursten, som i de japanska badrummen, eller med stearinljus och levande blommor, som i arabiska badrum.

Eftersom de här tendenserna har börjat spridas till resten av världen har inredningsarkitekter och arkitekter börjat lägga mer kraft på badrummens utseende. Ett bra exempel hittar vi i designen av badkar och speglar av Jaime Hayón för den spanska firman Artquitect, eller i de ovala badkar som designats av Ross Lovegrove för Vitra.

Tekniken har naturligtvis också fått en större roll. Massageduschar för hemmabruk, jacuzzis, bastur och andra anläggningar för vattenterapi finns nu till ett pris som många har råd med.

Nu för tiden finns det en oändlig variation av material för badrum. Marmorn har fortfarande en särställning, särskilt i elegantare badrum, och även om glas och trä har ökat är det svårt att föreställa sig att de någonsin kan överträffa elegansen hos badrum med keramik på väggar och golv.

Trä vittnar om kvalitet och vissa varianter, som teak, är att föredra eftersom de är mer vattentåliga. Små kakelplattor med glasmosaik bidrar med färg och struktur och kan användas till att täcka ett helt utrymme (golv och väggar) eller som en detalj (till exempel för att täcka utsidan av badkaret). Metaller och plastmaterial är vattenmotståndiga och används allt mer i designen av moderna badrum. Till och med målarfärger som tål vatten kan, rätt använda, ge en färgklick, förutsatt att badrummet är väl ventilerat.

Trots variationen i aktuella tendenser är minimalismen fortfarande ledande. Minimalistiska badrum följer principen "ju mindre desto bättre", framför allt när det gäller ljus och utrymme. Ett av de vanligaste valen är inredning i vit keramik och glas, marmor eller kromat stål för tillbehör och annat. Linjerna är enkla och utan utsmyckningar. Handdukar och andra badrumsföremål förvaras i inbyggda skåp och kommoder så att inget stör synintrycket eller symmetrin i badrummet.

Den exakta motsatsen, maximalismen, har också börjat slå igenom med stor kraft i badrumsdesignen. Maximalistiska utrymmen är imponerande, färggranna, med metallutsmyckningar och rundade och böljande former. Ofta inspireras man av inredningar från 1700- och 1800-talet. Maximalismen möjliggör en mer blandad och personlig stil.

Naturligtvis finns det en mängd varianter mellan de här två ytterligheterna. Det är bara att utforska begränsningarna för utrymmet som ska inredas, tänka på budgeten och, framför allt, ge fantasin fritt spelrum för att skapa ett badrum som blir till ens egen avskilda tillflyktsort.

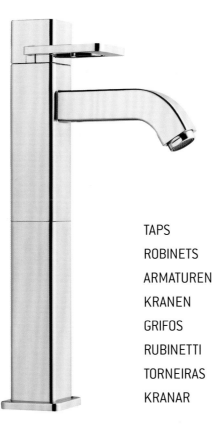

TAPS
ROBINETS
ARMATUREN
KRANEN
GRIFOS
RUBINETTI
TORNEIRAS
KRANAR

Combine the washbasin and taps in a similar style, since both will determine the design of the entire bathroom.

Combinez votre lavabo avec un robinet de style similaire, car ces deux éléments détermineront le style de votre salle de bains.

Waschbecken und Armaturen sollten in einem ähnlichen Stil kombiniert werden, da diese beiden Elemente den Stil des Bads bestimmen.

Combineer wastafels en kranen in dezelfde stijl, want deze twee onderdelen bepalen de gehele stijl van de badkamer.

Combina lavabos y grifería de estilo similar, ya que estos dos elementos determinarán el estilo del baño.

Combinate lavabi e rubinetterie di stile simile: questi due elementi determineranno lo stile del bagno.

Combine lavatórios e torneiras de estilo semelhante, já que estes dois elementos determinarão o estilo da casa de banho.

Välj tvättställ och kran i liknande stil, eftersom de kommer att lägga grunden för stilen på badrummet.

Select different finishes. The most common are chrome coupled with porcelain or glass handles.

Vous avez le choix entre différentes finitions comme par exemple, parmi les plus courantes, un robinet avec une finition chromée, une poignée en porcelaine ou en verre.

Man kann sich für unterschiedliche Oberflächenbehandlungen entscheiden, die geläufigsten sind die verchromten, mit Griffen aus Porzellan oder Kristall.

Je kunt kiezen voor verschillende uitvoeringen. Meestal wordt gekozen voor een chromen uitvoering met porseleinen of glazen handvaten.

Puedes elegir entre diferentes acabados: los más habituales son los cromados, con manija de porcelana o cristal.

Potete scegliere diverse rifiniture: le più consuete sono quelle cromate con maniglia di porcellana o vetro.

É possível escolher entre diferentes acabamentos; os mais habituais são os cromados, com punho de porcelana ou cristal.

Man kan välja olika ytbeläggning, men det vanligaste är krom med handtag i porslin eller glas.

Taps can be installed in one of
two ways : wall models or built-in
models.

Deux types d'installation sont
possibles, murale ou encastrée.

Man kann aus zwei Optionen
der Wasserhahninstallation
auswählen, es gibt Wandmodelle
oder eingebaute Modelle.

Er zijn twee mogelijkheden om
kranen te installeren: er bestaan
modellen die aan de muur worden
bevestigd en modellen die in de
wasbak zijn geïntegreerd.

Se puede escoger entre dos
opciones de instalación de la
grifería: modelos de pared o
modelos empotrados.

È possibile scegliere tra due
modalità d'installazione dei
rubinetti: modelli a parete o a
muro.

Pode-se escolher entre dois
sistemas de instalação das
torneiras, modelos de parede ou
modelos embutidos.

Det finns två valmöjligheter
för monteringen av blandare:
modeller med synlig kran och
inbyggda modeller.

Avoid models that require
uncomfortable postures or that
splash. Remember that taps must
be at the correct height.

Évitez de choisir un modèle qui
vous oblige à vous contorsionner
et occasionne des éclaboussures.
Rappelez-vous que les robinets
doivent être placés à une hauteur
confortable.

Es sollten Modelle vermieden
werden, die unbequeme
Stellungen verursachen oder
bei denen das Wasser spritzt.
Auch sollten die Armaturen eine
angemessene Höhe haben.

Vermijd modellen die ervoor
zorgen dat in je een verkeerde
houding staat of die te veel
spatten. Kranen moeten altijd op
de juiste hoogte worden bevestigd.

Evita modelos que ocasionen
posturas incómodas y
salpicaduras. Recuerda que los
grifos deben tener una altura
adecuada.

Evitate modelli che provochino
posture scomode e schizzi.
Ricordatevi che i rubinetti devono
essere posti ad un'altezza adatta.

Evite modelos que ocasionem
posições incómodas e salpicos.
Lembre-se de que as torneiras
devem ter uma altura adequada.

Undvik modeller som kräver
obekväma ställningar eller som
stänker mycket. Kom ihåg att
kranen ska sitta i rätt höjd.

Make sure that the tap has water
and energy control features.

Assurez-vous que le robinet
dispose d'un dispositif de contrôle
de l'eau et de l'énergie.

Man sollte darauf achten, dass die
Armatur Steuerungsapparaturen
für Wasser und Energie hat.

Zorg ervoor dat de kraan
voorzien is van een spaarkop
waarmee de watertoevoer en
het energiegebruik gereguleerd
kunnen worden.

Asegúrate de que el grifo disponga
de dispositivos de control de agua
y energía.

Assicuratevi che il rubinetto sia
dotato di dispositivi di controllo di
acqua ed energia.

Assegure-se de que a torneira
disponha de dispositivos de
controlo de água e energia.

Försäkra dig om att blandaren
ger möjlighet att kontrollera
vattenmängd och energi.

Select automatic electronic taps
that operate with a sensor for
enhanced hygiene and water
savings.

Choisissez des robinets
électroniques automatiques, qui
fonctionnent avec un capteur,
pour une meilleure hygiène et une
économie d'eau.

Automatische, elektronische
Wasserhähne, die mit einem
Sensor funktionieren, sind eine
gute Wahl, da sie hygienischer
sind und Wasser sparen.

Kies je voor een zo groot
mogelijke hygiëne en wil je zo veel
mogelijk water besparen, neem
dan een automatische, elektrische
kraan die met een sensor wordt
bediend.

Opta por griferías electrónicas
automáticas que funcionen con
un sensor para conseguir mayor
higiene y ahorro de agua.

Scegliete le rubinetterie
elettroniche automatiche con
sensore per ottenere maggiore
igiene e risparmio d'acqua.

Opte por torneiras eletrónicas
automáticas que funcionem com
um sensor para conseguir maior
higiene e poupança de água.

Välj gärna automatiska
elektroniska blandare med sensor
för bästa möjliga hygien och för
att spara vatten.

Some models come with state-of-the-art technologies that regulate the water output with the use of flow restrictors.

Il existe des modèles dotés d'une technologie avancée qui régulent le débit d'eau grâce à un régulateur d'intensité.

Es gibt Modelle mit modernen Technologien, die den Wasserfluss mit Intensitätsbegrenzern regulieren.

Er zijn modellen waarmee de kracht van de waterstraal door hoogstaande technologie wordt begrensd.

Existen modelos con tecnologías avanzadas que regulan el caudal de agua con limitadores de intensidad.

Esistono modelli tecnologicamente avanzati che regolano la portata d'acqua con limitatori d'intensità.

Existem modelos com tecnologias avançadas que regulam o caudal de água com limitadores de intensidade.

Det finns modeller med avancerad teknologi som reglerar vattenmängden och vattentrycket.

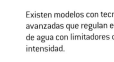

Thermostatic taps allow regulation of the water temperature beforehand.

Les robinets thermostatiques permettent de sélectionner au préalable une température qui sera constante à chaque utilisation.

Die Thermostat-Armaturen erlauben beim Öffnen die Auswahl einer konstanten Temperatur.

Met thermostaatkranen kan de temperatuur van het water van tevoren worden ingesteld. Deze temperatuur blijft constant telkens wanneer de kraan wordt geopend.

Los grifos termostáticos permiten preseleccionar una temperatura constante cada vez que se abren.

I rubinetti termostatici consentono di preselezionare una temperatura costante ogni volta che vengono aperti.

As torneiras termostáticas permitem pré-selecionar uma temperatura constante de cada vez que se abrem.

Blandare med termostat gör att man kan ställa in samma temperatur varje gång man vrider på kranen.

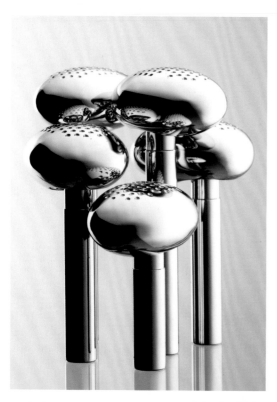

IB RUBINETTERIE
© IB Rubinetterie

VITRA
© Vitra

GRAFF FAUCETS
© Graff Faucets

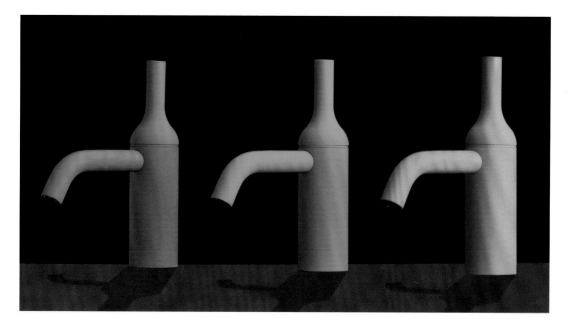

IB RUBINETTERIE
© IB Rubinetterie

GRAFF FAUCETS
© Graff Faucets

ZAZZERI
© Zazzeri

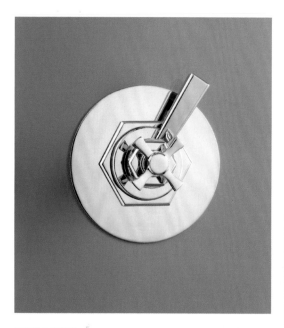

DEVON & DEVON
© Devon & Devon

KWC
© KWC

KWC
© KWC

KWC
© KWC

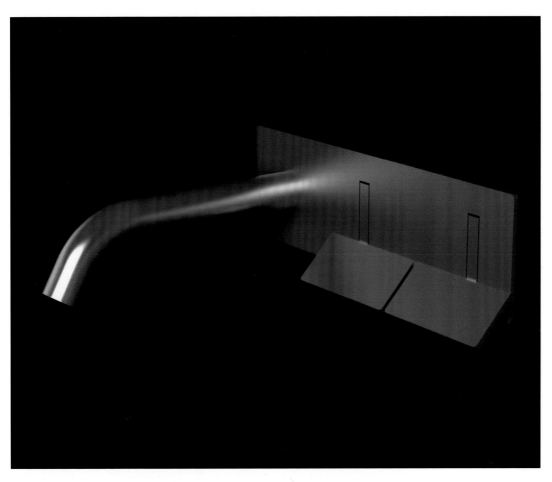

BOFFI
© Boffi

GRAFF FAUCETS
© Graff Faucets

© José Luis Hausmann

DEVON & DEVON
© Devon & Devon

DEVON & DEVON
© Devon & Devon

DEVON & DEVON
© Devon & Devon

WASHBASINS
LAVABOS
WASCHBECKEN
WASBAKKEN
LAVAMANOS
LAVABO
LAVATÓRIO
TVÄTTSTÄLL

When selecting a model, think about how it will be used and the visual impact it will create.

Au moment de choisir un modèle, vous devrez prendre en compte l'usage que vous en ferez ainsi que l'impact visuel recherché.

Bei der Auswahl sollte man berücksichtigen, welchen optischen und praktischen Nutzen das Möbel haben sollte.

Bij het uitkiezen van het model is het belangrijk om stil te staan bij het gebruik en de uitstraling ervan op het ontwerp.

A la hora de escoger el modelo deberemos considerar el uso que se dará al mueble y el impacto visual deseado.

Al momento della scelta del modello, sarà necessario considerare l'uso che si vuol fare del mobile e l'impatto visivo desiderato.

Na altura de escolher o modelo, devemos considerar o uso que se dará ao móvel e o impacto visual desejado.

När det är dags att välja modell ska man tänka över hur det ska användas och vilket estetiskt intryck man vill att det ger.

There are countless finishes to choose from including glazed porcelain, refractory clay, stainless steel and wrought iron.

Il existe un large choix de finitions comme la porcelaine vitrifiée, l'argile réfractaire, l'acier inoxydable ou encore la fonte.

Es gibt unzählige Optionen für die Oberflächengestaltung, wie zum Beispiel verglastes Porzellan, feuerfester Ton, Edelstahl oder Gusseisen.

Er zijn talrijke afwerkingen mogelijk, zoals verglaasd porselein, vuurvaste klei, roestvrij staal en smeedijzer.

Existen innumerables opciones de acabados tales como la porcelana vitrificada, la arcilla refractaria, el acero inoxidable o el hierro fundido.

Esistono innumerevoli opzioni per le rifiniture come, ad esempio, la porcellana vetrificata, l'argilla refrattaria, l'acciaio inox o la ghisa grigia.

Existem inúmeras opções de acabamentos, tais como a porcelana vitrificada, a argila refratária, o aço inoxidável ou o ferro fundido.

Det finns en mängd ytmaterial som glaserat porslin, eldfast keramik, rostfritt stål och järn.

Washbasins come in shapes to
suit all tastes and needs: square,
rectangular, round, oval, polygonal
and conical. Corner washbasins
are also available.

En termes de formes, il y en a
pour tous les goûts et pour tous
les besoins : des lavabos carrés,
rectangulaires, ronds, ovales, en
forme de polygones ou de cônes.

Formen gibt es für jeden
Geschmack, ob quadratisch,
rechteckig, rund, oval, polygon,
konisch oder eckig.

Wasbakken zijn er in alle vormen
en maten en voor alle smaken en
behoeften: vierkant, rechthoekig,
rond, ovaal, veelhoekig,
kegelvormig en er zijn speciale
hoekmodellen.

En cuanto a las formas, las
hay para todos los gustos
y necesidades: cuadradas,
rectangulares, redondas, ovaladas,
poligonales o cónicas.

Per quanto riguarda le forme, ce
n'è per tutti i gusti ed esigenze:
quadrati, rettangolari, rotondi,
ovali, a forma di poligono o conici.

Quanto às formas, existem para
todos os gostos e necessidades:
quadrados, retangulares,
redondos, ovalados, em forma de
polígonos ou cónicos.

Det finns former för alla smaker
och alla behov: kvadratiska,
rektangulära, runda, ovala,
månghörningar, konformade och
hörnanpassade.

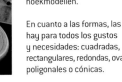

Built-in washbasins are a practical
choice in smaller bathrooms. The
space below it can be used for
storage.

Si votre salle de bains est petite, il
vaut mieux opter pour un lavabo
encastré. Cela vous permettra
d'utiliser le meuble du lavabo
comme espace de rangement.

Bei einem kleinen Bad ist das
eingebaute Waschbecken die
beste Lösung. Auf diese Weise
kann man den Raum darin nutzen,
Sachen zu verstauen.

Heb je een kleine badkamer, dan
kun je het best kiezen voor een
ingebouwd wasmeubel. Zo houd je
de meeste ruimte over om spullen
op te bergen.

Si dispones de un baño pequeño,
la mejor opción será un
lavamanos empotrado. Así podrás
aprovechar el espacio inferior para
almacenar enseres.

Nei bagni stretti, l'opzione ideale
sarà un lavabo del tipo modulo
con cassetti estraibili. Così potrete
approffitare lo spazio sottostante
per conservare oggetti.

Se dispusermos de uma casa de
banho pequena, a melhor opção
será um lavatório embutido.
Assim, pode-se aproveitar o
espaço inferior para armazenar os
utensílios.

Om du har ett litet badrum kan ett
tvättställ med kommod vara det
bästa alternativet. På det sättet
kan du utnyttja utrymmet under
tvättstället för förvaring.

In more narrow bathrooms, the
ideal choice is a module-style
washbasin with pull-out drawers.

Pour les salles de bains étroites,
il vaut mieux choisir un lavabo
de type meuble avec tiroirs
coulissants.

In engen Bädern ist die ideale
Option oft ein Waschbecken mit
einem Modul aus Schubfächern.

In smalle badkamers kun je het
best een wasmeubel installeren
met uitschuifbare lades.

En baños estrechos, la opción
ideal será un lavamanos tipo
módulo con cajones extraíbles.

Nei bagni stretti, l'opzione ideale
sarà un lavabo del tipo modulo
con cassetti estraibili.

Em casas de banho estreitas, a
opção ideal será um lavatório
tipo módulo com gavetas de
extrair.

I långsmala badrum är det
perfekt att ha ett tvättställ av
modultyp med utdragbara lådor.

Bathroom fixtures can be reused
when remodelling your bathroom,
as long as they don't exhibit any
cracks.

Au moment de rénover votre salle
de bains, vous pouvez toujours
réutiliser des éléments sanitaires
qui sont encore en bon état.

Wenn man das Bad neu gestaltet,
kann man die Sanitärgegenstände
erneut wiederverwenden, solange
sie heile sind.

Ga je de badkamer renoveren, dan
kun je onderdelen die nog heel zijn
hergebruiken.

A la hora de remodelar el baño,
puedes reutilizar piezas sanitarias
siempre que no presenten
fracturas.

Al momento di ristrutturare il
bagno potete riutilizzare i sanitari
a patto che non presentino
fratture.

Na altura de remodelar a casa
de banho, é possível reutilizar
peças sanitárias sempre que não
apresentem fraturas.

När badrummet ska renoveras
kan man återanvända
sanitetsporslinet förutsatt att det
inte finns sprickor i det.

If you have an antique vanity
cabinet at home, you can install
the washbasin in it, creating
a bathroom filled with rustic charm.

Si vous possédez un meuble
ancien, vous pouvez vous en
servir comme base pour y placer
le lavabo. Ainsi, vous obtiendrez
un lavabo dont le charme rustique
vous enchantera.

Wenn man im Haus ein altes
Möbelstück hat, kann dies auch
als Basis für ein Waschbecken
dienen. Dadurch wird das Bad
rustikaler und charmanter.

Heb je een oud meubelstuk in
huis? Dan kan deze dienen als
basis om de wasbak in te bouwen.
Zo krijgt hij een heel charmante,
rustieke uitstraling.

Si tenemos un mueble antiguo en
casa puede servirnos como base
para colocar el lavamanos. Con
ello conseguiremos un lavabo
rústico con mucho encanto.

Se possediamo un mobile antico
in casa, esso potrà servirci come
base per posizionare il lavabo. In
questo modo otterremo un lavabo
rustico affascinante.

Se tivermos um móvel antigo em
casa, pode servir-nos como base
para colocar o lavatório. Com
isso, conseguiremos um lavatório
rústico com muita graça.

Om du har en gammal möbel i
hemmet kan du använda den som
bas för handfatet. Du får ett rustikt
tvättställ med mycket charm.

Some modules couple ceramic
and sustainable materials, like
bamboo.

Il existe des modules alliant
céramique et matériaux durables,
comme le bambou par exemple.

Es gibt Module, die Keramik
mit nachhaltigen Materialien
kombinieren, wie zum Beispiel mit
Bambus.

Er bestaan meubels waarin
keramiek wordt gecombineerd
met duurzaam materiaal, zoals
bamboe.

Existen módulos que combinan
cerámica con materiales
sostenibles como el bambú.

Esistono moduli che combinano
ceramica con materiali sostenibili
come il bambù.

Existem módulos que combinam
cerâmica com materiais
sustentáveis, como o bambu.

Det finns moduler som
kombinerar keramik med
miljövänliga material, som bambu.

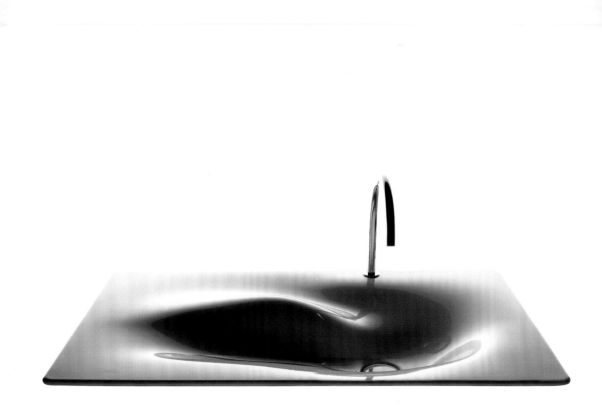

KANERA
© Kanera

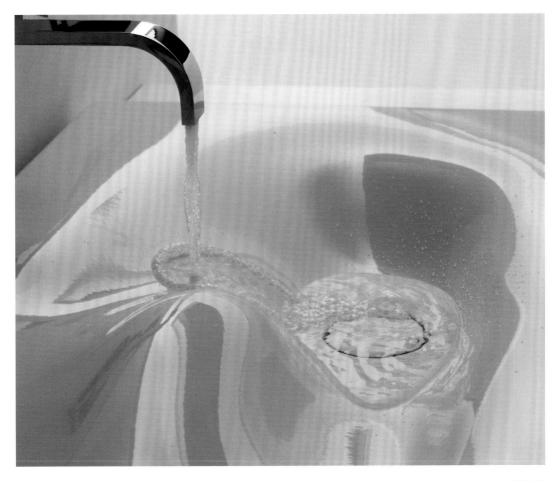

KANERA

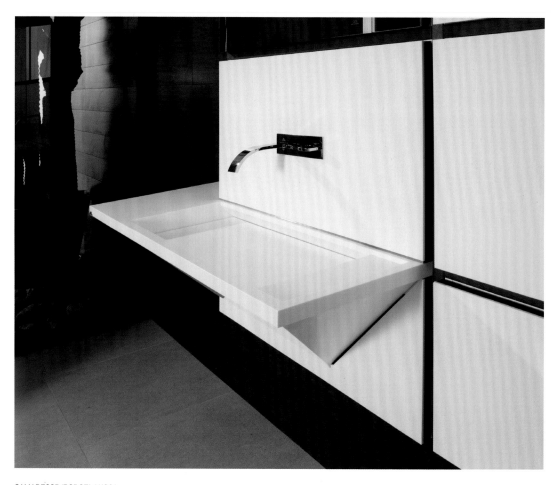

GAMADECOR/PORCELANOSA
© Gamadecor/Porcelanosa

GAMADECOR/PORCELANOSA
© Gamadecor/Porcelanosa

© José Luis Hausmann

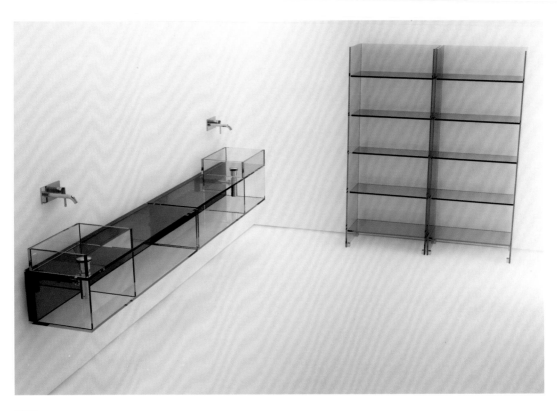

BOFFI
© Boffi

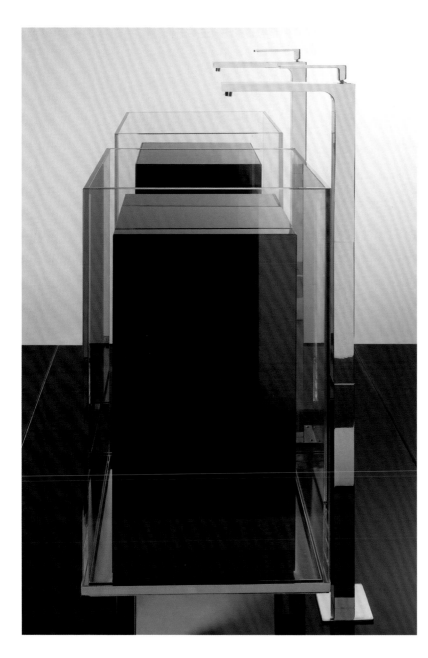

FRANCESC RIFÉ FOR © INBANI
© Francesc Rifé for © Inbani

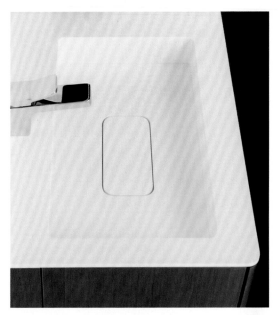

FRANCESC RIFÉ FOR © INBANI
© Francesc Rifé for © Inbani

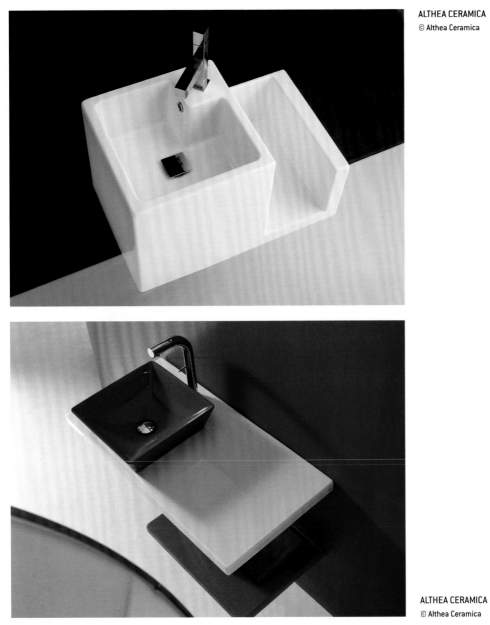

ALAPE
Insert
© Alape

ALAPE
Insert
© Alape

ARTCERAM
© Artceram

ARTCERAM
© Artceram

ARTCERAM
© Artceram

OLYMPIA CERAMICA
Ukiyo-Ɛ
© Olympia Ceramica

BETTE
© Bette

DEVON & DEVON
© Devon & Devon

ALTHEA CERAMICA

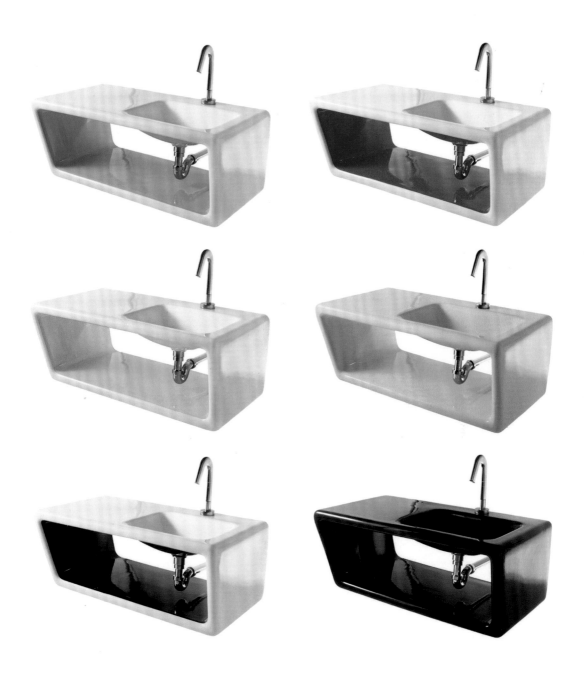

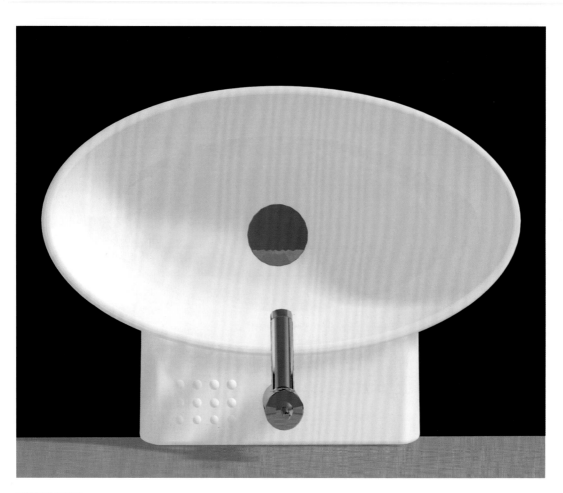

ALTHEA CERAMICA
© Althea Ceramica

ALTHEA CERAMICA
© Althea Ceramica

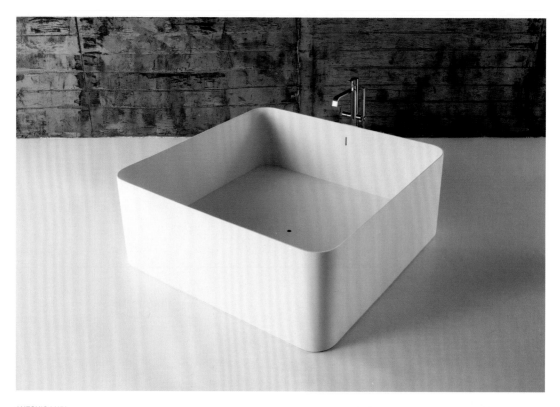

ANTONIO LUPI
© Antonio Lupi

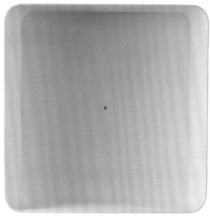

ANTONIO LUPI
© Antonio Lupi

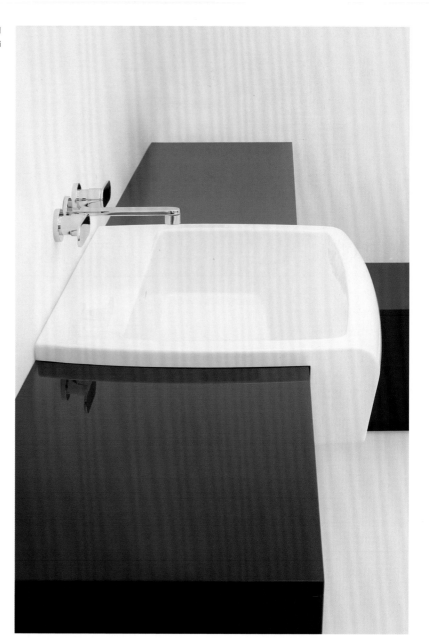

ALAPE
Tangens
© Alape

VILLEROY & BOCH
© Villeroy & Boch

VILLEROY & BOCH
© Villeroy & Boch

ANTONIO LUPI
© Antonio Lupi

BETTE
Monolith
© Bette

ANTONIO LUPI
© Antonio Lupi

BETTE
Relax Highline
© Bette

BETTE
Monolith
© Bette

BETTE
Monolith
© Bette

DEVON & DEVON
© Devon & Devon

DEVON & DEVON
© Devon & Devon

DEVON & DEVON
© Devon & Devon

DURAVIT
Onto
© Duravit

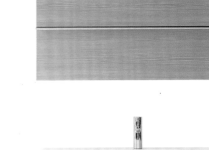

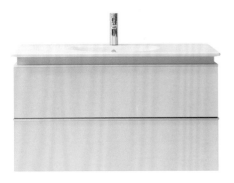

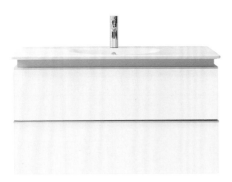

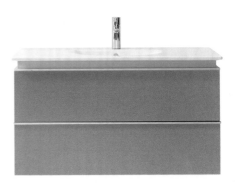

DURAVIT
Darling New
© Duravit

DURAVIT
Darling New
© Duravit

TOILETS AND BIDETS

TOILETTES ET BIDETS

KLOSETT UND BIDETS

WC'S EN BIDETS

INODOROS Y BIDÉS

WATER E BIDET

SANITAS E BIDÉS

TOALETTER OCH BIDÉER

When selecting toilets and bidets, bear in mind their comfort and functionality.

Au moment de choisir les éléments sanitaires, vous devez tenir compte du confort et de la fonctionnalité des éléments.

Bei der Auswahl der Sanitärgegenstände muss man sich den Komfort und die Funktionalität der Teile vor Augen halten.

Bij het uitkiezen van een wc, moet vooral gedacht worden aan het zitcomfort en de functionaliteit ervan.

Cuando escojamos los sanitarios, deberemos tener en cuenta el confort y la funcionalidad de las piezas.

Quando scegliamo i sanitari, dovremmo prendere in considerazione il comfort e la funzionalità dei pezzi.

Quando escolhemos os artigos sanitários, devemos ter em conta o conforto e a funcionalidade das peças.

När man ska välja sanitetsporslin ska man tänka på komfort och funktionalitet.

A range of models with different positions are available. For a greater sense of stability, select standing toilets and bidets.

Il existe différents modèles selon l'emplacement désiré. Si vous cherchez à privilégier la stabilité, mieux vaut choisir des toilettes classiques.

Bei verschiedenen Modellen kommt es auf die Position an. Ein Standgerät wirkt dabei wesentlich stabiler.

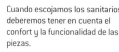

Er zijn verschillende soorten modellen. Wie stevig wil zitten, kan het best kiezen voor een staande toiletpot.

Existen diferentes modelos por lo que respecta a la posición. Si queremos proporcionar mayor sensación de estabilidad, optaremos por sanitarios de pie.

Esistono vari modelli rispetto alla posizione. Se vogliamo offrire una maggiore sensazione di stabilità, sceglieremo dei sanitari da terra.

Existem diferentes modelos no que se refere à posição. Se quisermos proporcionar maior sensação de estabilidade, devemos optar por artigos sanitários com pé.

Det finns olika modeller för olika placeringar. Om känslan av stabilitet är det viktigaste, ska man ta toalettstolar på fot.

Wall-hung toilets and bidets offer substantial space savings and are aesthetically pleasing.

Si le but est de libérer l'espace, tant au niveau physique que visuel, choisissez des toilettes suspendues.

Hängende Sanitäranlage geben dem Raum mehr Leichtigkeit.

Wie de beschikbare ruimte zo open mogelijk wil houden, kan beter kiezen voor een hangende toiletpot.

Si lo que buscamos es aligerar el espacio física y visualmente optaremos por sanitarios suspendidos.

Se quello che cerchiamo è alleggerire lo spazio sia fisicamente che visualmente, sceglieremo dei sanitari sospesi.

Se o que procuramos é aligeirar o espaço físico e visualmente, devemos optar por artigos sanitários suspensos.

Om man istället vill ge badrummet en luftigare känsla och stil väljer man upphängd toalettstol.

Add colour to your bathroom by selecting details that bring the toilet or bidet to life.

Si vous désirez mettre de la couleur dans votre salle d'eau, il existe des accessoires de décor pour vos toilettes ou votre bidet.

Wenn man Farbe in die Toilette bringen möchte, kann man sich für lebhafte Details entscheiden und sie an der Zisterne.

Wie wat kleur wil brengen in het toilet kan kiezen voor details die de wc of het bidet levendiger maken.

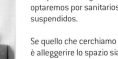

Si queremos introducir color en el aseo se puede optar por detalles que otorguen vida al inodoro o al bidé.

Se vogliamo dare un tocco di colore alla toilette, è possibile scegliere dettagli che vivacizzino il water o il bidet.

Se quisermos introduzir cor na casa de banho, podemos optar por detalhes que transmitam vida à sanita ou ao bidé.

Vill man ha färg i badrummet kan man välja detaljer som ger liv åt toaletten eller bidén.

Dual flush toilets help to lower water consumption. Building regulations in many countries require them to be installed.

Les chasses d'eau à double poussoir permettent de réduire la consommation d'eau. Les normes de construction de nombreux pays imposent ce type d'installation.

Die Entladungen mit doppeltem Druckknopf senken den Wasserverbrauch und sind in den meisten Ländern Pflicht.

Met reservoirs met een dubbele spoelknop kan het watergebruik worden teruggedrongen. In veel landen wordt de installatie van zulke reservoirs wettelijk voorgeschreven.

Las descargas de doble pulsador permiten reducir el consumo de agua. La normativa edificativa de muchos países exige su instalación.

Gli scarichi a doppio pulsante consentono di ridurre il consumo dell'acqua. La normativa di costruzione in vigore in molti Paesi ne richiede l'installazione.

Os autoclismos de botão duplo permitem reduzir o consumo de água. A normativa de construção de muitos países exige a sua instalação.

Dubbla spolknappar gör det möjligt att minska vattenkonsumtionen. Byggnadslagarna i de flesta länder kräver att sådana används.

A volume control is a simple, inexpensive device that helps to save water in toilet tanks.

Le réducteur de volume d'eau est un dispositif simple et peu coûteux qui, placé dans le bac d'eau des WC, permet de réduire la consommation d'eau.

Der Mengenreduzierer ist eine einfache und kostengünstige Apparatur, um Wasser in den WC-Systemen zu sparen.

Door een goede afstelling van het spoelmechanisme kan op een eenvoudige en goedkope manier water worden bespaard.

El reductor volumétrico es un dispositivo sencillo y de bajo coste que contribuye al ahorro de agua en las cisternas de WC.

Il riduttore di volume è un dispositivo semplice ed economico che contribuisce al risparmio di acqua nelle vasche di scarico.

O redutor volumétrico é um dispositivo simples e de baixo custo que contribui para a poupança de água nos autoclismos de WC.

En vattensparare är en enkel och billig anordning som bidrar till att spara vatten i toalettcisterner.

Heated seats, automatic bidet features, antibacterial materials: the advances and applications are infinite.

Les sièges chauffants ou motorisés, les chasses d'eau automatiques, les matériaux antibactériens : les progrès et les nouvelles applications qui en découlent sont sans limites.

Sitze mit Heizung, mit Motoren, automatische Spritzdüsen, antibakterielle Materialien: der Fortschritt geht weiter und die Anwendungen sind unendlich.

De vooruitgang en de toepassingen lijken geen grenzen meer te kennen: verwarmde toiletbrillen, toiletbrillen die automatisch gereinigd worden, elektronisch gestuurde waterstralen, antibacterieel materiaal...

Asientos con calefacción o motorizados, chorros automáticos, materiales antibacterianos: los avances y las aplicaciones son infinitas.

Sedili con riscaldamento o motorizzati, getti automatici, materiali antibatterici: i progressi e le applicazioni sono infinite.

Assentos com aquecimento ou motorizados, jatos automáticos, materiais antibacterianos: os avanços e aplicações são infinitos.

Uppvärmda sitsar, motoriserade sitsar, automatisk spolning, antibakteriella material... Framstegen och valmöjligheterna är oändliga.

For the more ecologically-minded, self-composting toilets are available that use not water but warm air to decompose the waste.

Pour les plus exigeants, il existe des toilettes sèches qui utilisent non de l'eau mais de l'air chaud pour la décomposition des excréments.

Für Personen mit höchstem Anspruch gibt es auch Toiletten, die automatisch kompostieren und die statt Wasser heiße Luft verwenden, um den Stuhl zu zersetzen.

Er bestaan ook zelfcomposterende wc's die geen water verbruiken, maar waarin uitwerpselen worden afgebroken door warme lucht.

Para los más exigentes, existen retretes autocompostables que no utilizan agua sino aire caliente para descomponer las heces.

Per i più esigenti, esistono WC autocompostabili che non utilizzano acqua ma aria calda per decomporre le feci.

Para os mais exigentes, existem sanitas autocompensáveis que não utilizam água, mas ar quente para decompor as fezes.

För de platser som kräver det, finns det toaletter som inte använder vatten utan varmluft för att ta hand om avföringen.

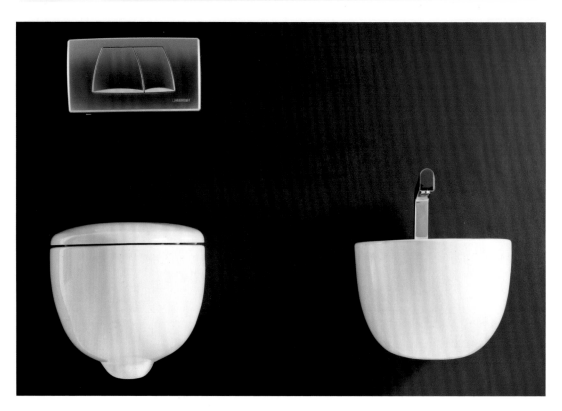

ALTHEA CERAMICA
© Althea Ceramica

ALTHEA CERAMICA
© Althea Ceramica

ALTHEA CERAMICA
© Althea Ceramica

PHILIPPE STARK FOR © DURAVIT
© Philippe Stark for © Duravit

ALTHEA CERAMICA
© Althea Ceramica

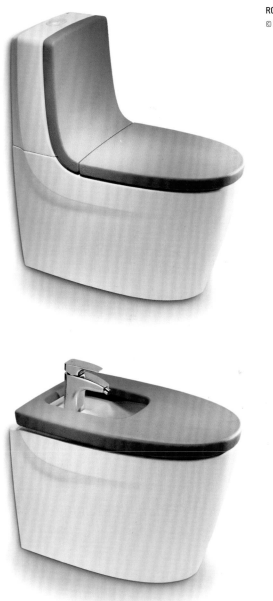

CERAMICA FLAMINIA
© Ceramica Flaminia

ALTHEA CERAMICA
© Althea Ceramica

PORCELANOSA
© Porcelanosa

ALTHEA CERAMICA
© Althea Ceramica

GRUP GAMMA
© Grup Gamma

DURAVIT
© Duravit

ANTONIO LUPI
© Antonio Lupi

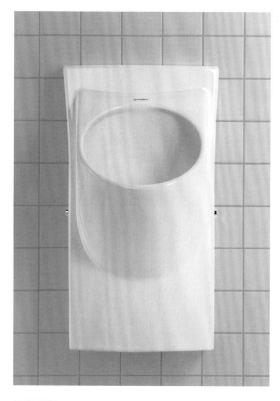

ARTQUITECT
© Artquitect

DURAVIT
© Duravit

PHILIPPE STARK FOR © DURAVIT
© Philippe Stark for © Duravit

PHILIPPE STARK FOR © DURAVIT
© Philippe Stark for © Duravit

ALESSI
© Alessi

PHILIPPE STARK FOR © DURAVIT
Senso Wash
© Philippe Stark for © Duravit

PHILIPPE STARK FOR © DURAVIT
Senso Wash
© Philippe Stark for © Duravit

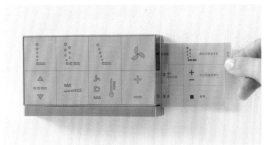

PHILIPPE STARK FOR © DURAVIT
Senso Wash
© Philippe Stark for © Duravit

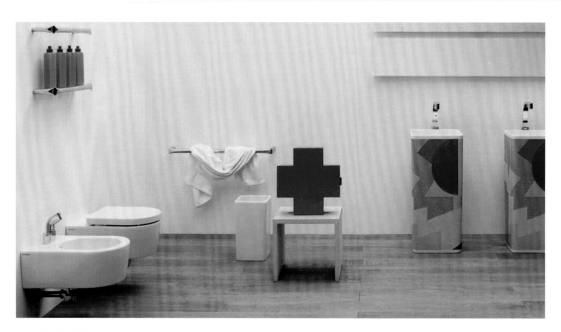

CERAMICA FLAMINIA
© Ceramica Flaminia

CERAMICA FLAMINIA
© Ceramica Flaminia

YANKO DESIGN
Universal Toilet
© Yanko Design

ALESSI
© Alessi

© Jordi Miralles

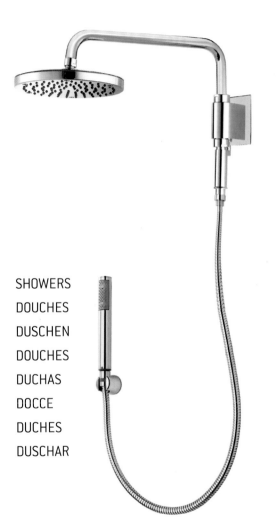

SHOWERS
DOUCHES
DUSCHEN
DOUCHES
DUCHAS
DOCCE
DUCHES
DUSCHAR

More and more people are deciding to remove the bathtub and install a shower. This lowers water consumption and takes up less space.

De plus en plus de gens choisissent de remplacer leur baignoire par une douche. Cela permet de réduire la consommation d'eau et de gagner de l'espace.

Viele entscheiden sich gegen eine Badewanne und für eine Dusche, damit sich der Wasserverbrauch reduziert und mehr Platz da ist.

Steeds meer mensen besluiten de badkuip te vervangen door een douche. Daarmee besparen ze water en ruimte.

Cada vez son más las personas que se deciden por quitar la bañera y poner una ducha. El consumo de agua se reduce y se ahorra espacio.

Sono sempre di più le persone che decidono di togliere la vasca da bagno e installare una doccia. Il consumo di acqua si riduce e si risparmia spazio.

Cada vez são mais as pessoas que se decidem por tirar a banheira e colocar um duche. O consumo de água reduz-se e poupa-se espaço.

Det är allt fler som väljer att ta bort badkaret och sätta in dusch. Vattenkonsumtionen minskar och man sparar utrymme.

There is a host of options when selecting a shower. Carefully measure the space you want it to occupy.

Au moment de choisir une douche, il y a un large éventail d'options. Mesurez bien l'espace dont vous disposez.

In dem Fall bietet eine Dusche viele Optionen. Man sollte den Raum gut bemessen, den die Dusche einnehmen soll.

Wie kiest voor een douche heeft veel mogelijkheden. Meet de ruimte die je ervoor wilt gebruiken goed op.

A la hora de elegir una ducha hay muchas opciones. Mide bien el espacio que quieres ocupar.

Quando si sceglie una doccia ci sono molte opzioni. Misurate bene lo spazio che volete occupare.

Na altura de escolher um duche há muitas opções. Meça bem o espaço que quer ocupar.

När det är dags att välja dusch har man många valmöjligheter. Mät det utrymme som du vill använda noggrant.

Many designs fit into areas with angles, although you can also choose round, square or rectangular bases.

De nombreux modèles s'adaptent aux zones anguleuses, bien que vous puissiez également opter pour un bac à douche rond, carré ou rectangulaire.

Viele Designs können in Bereichen mit Winkeln angepasst werden, obwohl man sich auch für runde, quadratische oder rechteckige Platten entscheiden kann.

Veel douches zijn ontworpen om in de hoek geplaatst te worden. Hoewel je ook kunt kiezen voor een ronde, vierkante of rechthoekige douchebak.

Muchos diseños se adaptan a las zonas donde hay ángulos, aunque puedes optar por platos redondos, cuadrados o rectangulares.

Molti modelli sono adatti a zone in cui ci sono angoli, anche se è possibile scegliere tra piatti rotondi, quadrati o rettangolari.

Muitos modelos adaptam-se a zonas onde há cantos, embora se possa optar por bases redondas, quadradas ou retangulares.

Många designer är anpassade för hörn, men man kan använda runda, fyrkantiga eller rektangulära utrymmen.

There are a wide range of predesigned bases available made of different materials, including acrylic, porcelain, steel, stoneware and tropical wood.

Vous pouvez choisir dans une large gamme de bacs préfabriqués, faits de matériaux divers comme l'acrylique, la porcelaine, l'acier, le grès ou encore le bois exotique.

Man kann aus vielen vordesignten Platten aus unterschiedlichen Materialien auswählen, ob aus preisgünstigem Acryl, Porzellan, Stahl, Sandstein oder Tropenholz.

Voor douchebakken kun je kiezen uit een breed palet van bestaande ontwerpen die zijn gemaakt van verschillende materialen, zoals acryl, porselein, staal, aardewerk of tropisch hardhout.

Puedes escoger entre una amplia gama de platos prediseñados y de diferentes materiales, como acrílicos, porcelana, acero, gres o madera tropical.

Potete scegliere tra un'ampia gamma di piatti pre-disegnati di diversi materiali, come acrilici, in porcellana, acciaio, gres o legno tropicale.

Pode escolher entre uma vasta gama de bases pré-desenhadas e de vários materiais, como acrílicos, porcelana, aço, grés ou madeira tropical.

Man kan välja bland ett stort utbud fördesignade duschkabiner av olika material som akryl, porslin, stål, stengods eller tropiska träslag.

If it's preferable for the shower base to be integrated into the surface; extra-thin bases can be installed at floor level.

Si vous désirez que le bac soit intégré au sol, il existe de nombreux bacs ultraplats qui peuvent être placés au ras du sol.

Wenn man möchte, dass sich die Platte in die Oberfläche einfügt, gibt es extra flache Platten, die knapp über der Bodenfläche abschließen.

Als je wilt dat de douchebak nagenoeg gelijk ligt aan het vloeroppervlak kun je kiezen voor een ultraplatte bak met een subtiel opstaande rand.

Si quieres que el plato quede integrado en la superficie, existen modelos extraplanos que quedan a ras del suelo.

Se volete che il piatto si inserisca nella superficie, scegliete modelli ultrasottili: rimangono a livello del pavimento.

Se quisermos que a base fique integrada na superfície, existem bases extraplanas que ficam ao nível do solo.

Vill man ha duschkabinen integrerad i utrymmet finns det extra tunna duschkabiner som ligger i nivå med golvet.

Choose the shower to suit your needs: with water massage, steam bath, benches to sit on or even a radio and telephone.

Choisissez la douche selon vos besoins : hydromassante, à vapeur, dotée d'un banc pour s'asseoir et même d'une radio et d'un téléphone.

Sucht man sich die Dusche nach seinen Bedürfnissen aus: mit Hydromassage, Dampfbad, mit Sitzbänken und sogar mit Radio und Telefon.

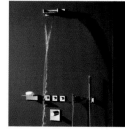

Kun je een douche uitkiezen die voorziet in al je behoeften: met hydromassage, stoombad, zitbanken en zelfs met ingebouwde radio en telefoon.

Elige la ducha en función de tus necesidades: con hidromasaje, baño de vapor, con bancos para sentarte e incluso con radio y teléfono.

Scegliete la doccia in base alle vostre necessità: con idromassaggio, bagno di vapore, con sedili per sedervi e addirittura con radio e telefono.

Escolha o duche em função das suas necessidades: com hidromassagem, banho de vapor, com bancos para sentar e até com rádio e telefone.

Väljer man dusch efter behov: med vattenmassage, ångdusch, sittbänk eller till och med radio eller telefon.

Installing a thermostatic mixer will automatically maintain the water at a constant temperature.

En y ajoutant un mitigeur thermostatique, vous pourrez maintenir une température constante de l'eau automatiquement.

Baut man noch einen Thermostatmischer ein, hilft dieser dabei, automatisch die Wassertemperatur zu halten.

Zorg ervoor dat er een thermosstatische mengkraan wordt geïnstalleerd waarmee je de temperatuur van het water automatisch constant houdt.

Incorpora un mezclador termostático, te ayudará a mantener constante la temperatura del agua de forma automática.

Aggiungete un miscelatore termostatico: vi aiuterà a mantenere costante la temperatura dell'acqua in modo automatico.

Incorpore um misturador termostático, que ajudará a manter constante a temperatura da água de forma automática.

Välj en blandare med termostat som hjälper dig att behålla en jämn vattentemperatur helt automatiskt.

Environmentally-friendly showers release negative ions which are highly beneficial to human health while also cleaning and toning the skin.

Il existe des écodouches qui libèrent des ions négatifs excellents pour la santé, ce qui nettoie et tonifie votre peau.

Es gibt Ökoduschen, die negative Ionen freisetzen, was sehr gesund ist, da sie gleichzeitig die Haut reinigen und festigen.

Er bestaan ook eco-douches die de negatieve ionen uit het water bevrijden. Deze zijn goed voor de gezondheid, want zonder dat er zeep gebruikt hoeft te worden.

Existen ecoduchas que liberan iones negativos muy beneficiosos para la salud, que a la vez limpian y tonifican la piel.

Esistono eco docce che rilasciano ioni negativi molto benefici per la salute e che allo stesso tempo puliscono e tonificano la pelle.

Existem duches ecológicos que libertam iões negativos muito benéficos para a saúde, ao mesmo tempo que limpam e tonificam a pele.

Det finns ekoduschar som släpper ut negativa joner som är mycket bra för hälsan samtidigt som de rengör och stärker huden utan att man behöver använda tvål.

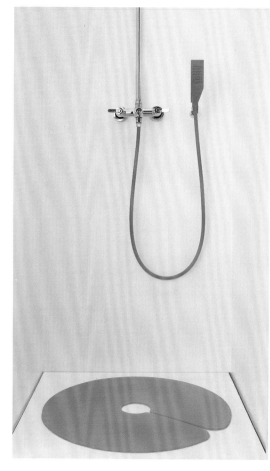

AGAPE
© Agape

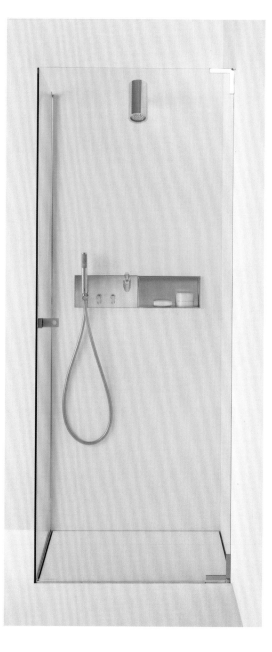

AGAPE
© Agape

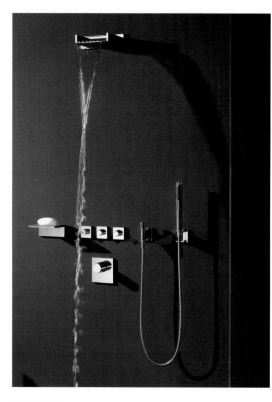

DORNBRACHT
© Dornbracht

HANSGROHE ESPAÑA
Axor Stark Collection
© Hansgrohe España

GALA
© Gala

JACLO
© Jaclo

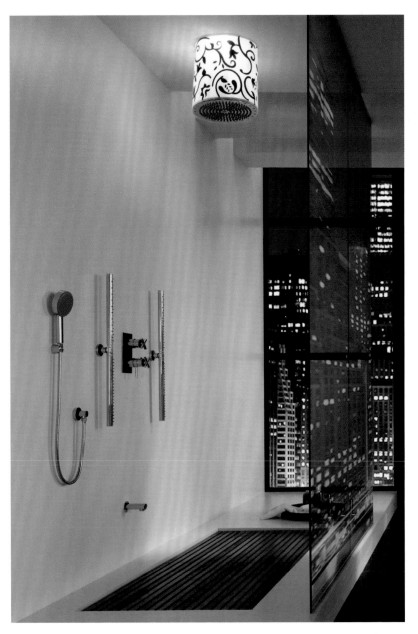

DORNBRACHT
© Dornbracht

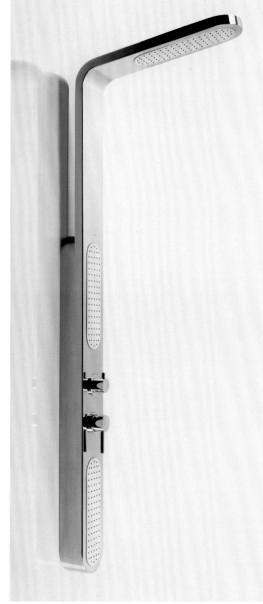

JACLO
© Jaclo

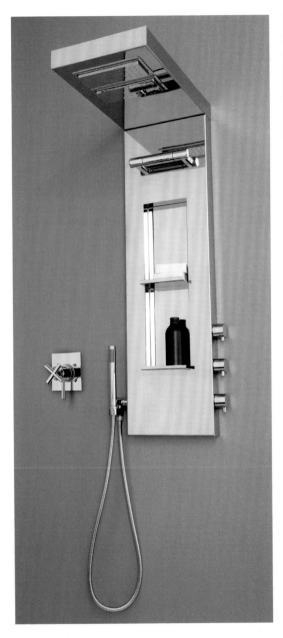

JACLO
© Jaclo

JACLO

© Jaclo

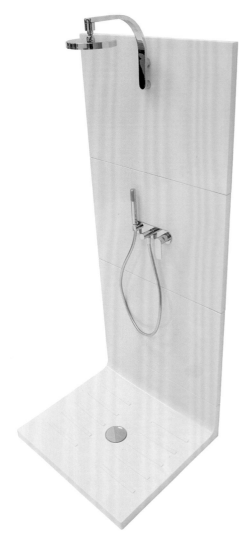

CERAMICA FLAMINIA
© Ceramica Flaminia

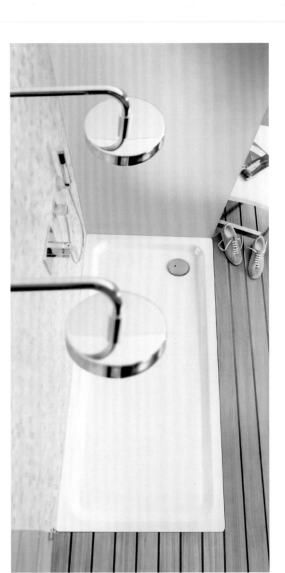

KALDEWEI
© Kaldewei

NEWFORM
© Newform

NEWFORM
© Newform

ALTHEA CERAMICA
© Althea Ceramica

© José Luis Hausmann

© José Luis Hausmann

KALDEWEI
© Kaldewei

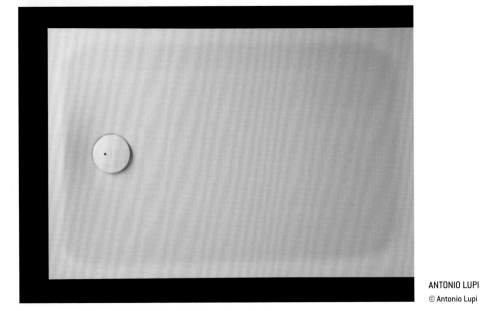

ANTONIO LUPI
© Antonio Lupi

BETTE
© Bette

BETTE
© Bette

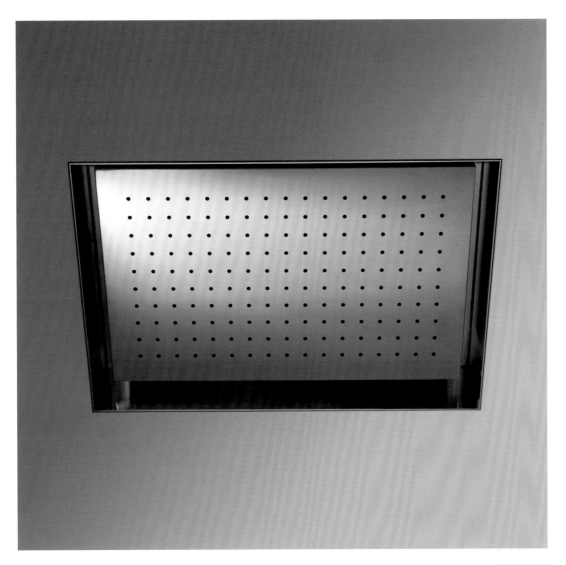

ANTONIO LUPI
© Antonio Lupi

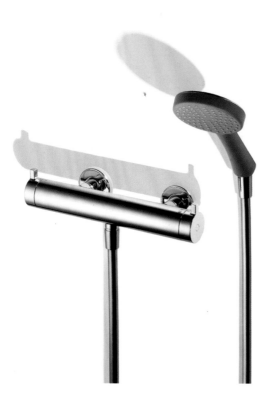

KWC
© KWC

KWC
© KWC

KWC
© KWC

BATHTUBS

BAIGNOIRES

BADEWANNEN

BADKUIPEN

BAÑERAS

VASCHE DA BAGNO

BANHEIRAS

BADKAR

It's important to select your bathtub carefully because there is such a wide variety of designs in terms of both size and shape.

Au moment de choisir une baignoire, il vaut mieux savoir ce que vous voulez, car le choix de designs, de tailles et de formes est vaste.

Die Auswahl der Badewanne muss gut überlegt sein, da es sie in vielen verschiedenen Formen und Größen gibt.

Kies uit de enorme verscheidenheid in design, grootte en vorm de juiste badkuip.

La elección de la bañera debe estar bien meditada, ya que hay una gran variedad de diseños tanto en tamaños como en formas.

La scelta della vasca da bagno deve essere ben meditata, dato che esiste una grande varietà di modelli sia per dimensioni che per forme.

A escolha da banheira deve ser bem pensada, já que existe uma grande variedade de modelos tanto em tamanhos como formas.

För badkar gäller det att göra ett klokt val, eftersom det finns en stor mängd olika stilar, storlekar och former.

Read up on the qualities of bathtub materials not only because of the effect of the finish but also because they directly affect quality.

Assurez-vous de bien connaître les caractéristiques du matériau qui compose la baignoire, non seulement pour le rendu de la finition mais aussi parce qu'il a une incidence directe sur sa qualité.

Man sollte sich gut über die Qualität des Materials der Badewanne informieren, auch hinsichtlich der Oberflächenbehandlung.

Informeer goed naar de eigenschappen van het materiaal waarvan de badkuip is gemaakt. Dat is niet alleen van invloed op de afwerking ervan, maar ook op de kwaliteit.

Infórmate bien de las cualidades del material, no solo por el efecto del acabado, sino también porque incide directamente en su calidad.

Informatevi bene riguardo alla qualità del materiale della vasca da bagno, non solo per l'effetto della finitura, ma anche perché influisce direttamente sulla sua qualità.

Informe-se bem das qualidades do material da banheira, não só pelo efeito do acabamento, mas também porque influencia diretamente a sua qualidade.

Ta reda på all information om kvaliteten på materialet i badkaret, inte bara för ytfinishens skull utan också för att det avslöjar badkarets kvalitet.

Acrylic bathtubs are the most inexpensive, although they are susceptible to cracks over a period of time, unlike other materials.

Les baignoires en acrylique sont les plus économiques bien qu'avec le temps, elles puissent se lézarder, ce qui ne se produit pas avec les autres matériaux.

Badewannen aus Acryl werden am häufigsten verwendet und sie sind preisgünstig. Sie können aber mit der Zeit Risse bekommen, was bei anderen Materialien nicht passiert.

Badkuipen van acryl komen het meest voor en zijn het goedkoopst. Maar na verloop van tijd kunnen er barsten in de kuip komen, iets dat met andere materialen niet het geval is.

Las bañeras acrílicas son las más económicas, aunque con el tiempo pueden agrietarse, algo que no sucede con otros materiales.

Le vasche da bagno acriliche sono le più economiche anche se con il tempo possono incrinarsi, cosa che non succede invece con altri materiali.

As banheiras acrílicas são as mais económicas, embora com o tempo possam rachar, algo que não sucede com outros materiais.

Badkar av akryl är vanligast och billigast men de kan med tiden få sprickor, vilket inte inträffar med andra material.

Steel bathtubs are a good choice since they readily adapt to changes in temperature and are easy to clean.

Les baignoires en acier constituent un bon choix, elles s'adaptent facilement aux changements de température et sont faciles à nettoyer.

Stahlbadewannen sind eine gute Wahl, da sie sich gut an Temperaturschwankungen anpassen und ihre Reinigung ist einfach.

Stalen badkuipen zijn een goede keus omdat die zich goed kunnen aanpassen aan temperatuurverschillen en eenvoudig schoon te houden zijn.

Las bañeras de acero son una buena elección ya que se adaptan muy bien a los cambios de temperatura y su limpieza es sencilla.

Le vasche in acciaio rappresentano una buona scelta perché si adattano molto bene ai cambiamenti di temperatura e la loro pulizia risulta semplice.

As banheiras de aço são uma boa escolha, pois adaptam-se muito bem às mudanças de temperatura e a sua limpeza é fácil.

Badkar av stål är ett bra val eftersom de anpassar sig mycket bra vid temperaturförändringar och är enkla att hålla rena.

Wrought iron bathtubs are
covered with an enamel glaze and
are very long-lasting.

Les baignoires en fonte sont
très résistantes car elles sont
recouvertes d'émail vitrifié.

Gusseiserne Badewannen sind
sehr haltbar, da sie mit verglaster
Emaille beschichtet sind.

Gietijzeren badkuipen zijn zeer
bestendig omdat ze bedekt zijn
met verglaasd email.

Las bañeras de fundición son
muy resistentes porque están
recubiertas de esmalte vitrificado.

Le vasche in ghisa sono molto
resistenti perché sono ricoperte di
smalto vetrificato.

As banheiras de ferro fundido são
muito resistentes porque são
recobertas por esmalte vitrificado.

Badkar i gjutjärn är mycket
tåliga eftersom de är täckta av
glasemalj.

Ceramic bathtubs are lovely but
extremely heavy and can crack
easily if something is dropped
on them.

Les baignoires en céramique
sont très belles mais aussi très
lourdes, et que la simple chute
d'un objet peut les abîmer.

Eine Keramikwanne ist zwar sehr
schön, aber auch zerbrechlich,
wenn etwas darauf fällt.

Keramieke badkuipen zijn erg
mooi, maar ook erg zwaar en ze
kunnen eenvoudig breken als er
iets op valt.

Las bañeras de cerámica son
muy bonitas pero también muy
pesadas, y pueden partirse
fácilmente si les cae un objeto.

Le vasche da bagno in ceramica
sono molto belle ma anche molto
pesanti, e possono rompersi
facilmente con la caduta di un
oggetto.

As banheiras de cerâmica
são muito bonitas, mas muito
pesadas e podem partir-se
facilmente se lhes cair em cima
algum objeto.

Om du föredrar badkar av
keramik är de mycket vackra
men också mycket tunga och
de spricker lätt om något faller
mot dem.

Bathtubs made from synthetic materials offer a range of bright colours and unique shapes.

Si vous recherchez des couleurs vives ou des formes variées, choisissez parmi les baignoires composées de matériaux synthétiques.

Wenn man nach schillernden Farben sucht oder sich für außergewöhnliche Formen interessiert, sollte man sich für eine Badewanne aus synthetischem Material entscheiden.

Gaat je voorkeur uit naar stralende kleuren of een andere vorm, kies dan voor een badkuip van synthetisch materiaal.

Si lo que buscas son colores brillantes o formas diferentes, opta por una bañera de materiales sintéticos.

Se quello che cercate sono colori brillanti o forme svariate, optate per una vasca in materiali sintetici.

Se o que procura são cores brilhantes ou com formas diferentes, opte por banheiras de materiais sintéticos.

Är du ute efter glada färger eller annorlunda former kan du välja ett badkar av syntetmaterial som tillverkas i gjutform och finns tillgängliga i originella designer.

Take into consideration your water consumption and you will discover positive factors for both your pocketbook and the environment.

Cependant, pensez à votre consommation d'eau et vous en découvrirez les aspects positifs, autant pour l'environnement que pour votre portefeuille.

Allerdings sollte man über seinen Wasserverbrauch nachdenken und dann wird man die positiven Aspekte erkennen, sowohl für seinen Geldbeutel als auch für die Umwelt.

Denk ook na over het watergebruik en vooral over de positieve aspecten, zowel voor je portemonnee als voor het milieu.

Sin embargo, reflexiona sobre tu consumo de agua y descubrirás los aspectos positivos tanto para tu bolsillo como para el medio ambiente.

Ad ogni modo, riflettete sul vostro consumo d'acqua e scoprirete i lati positivi sia per le vostre tasche che per l'ambiente.

No entanto, reflita sobre o seu consumo de água e descobrirá os aspetos positivos, tanto para a sua bolsa como para o meio ambiente.

Oavsett vilket ska du tänka noga på din vattenkonsumtion. Du kommer att upptäcka att det är bra för både plånboken och miljön.

KALDEWEI
© Kaldewei

AQUATIC INDUSTRIES
Serenity
© Aquatic Industries

KALDEWEI
© Kaldewei

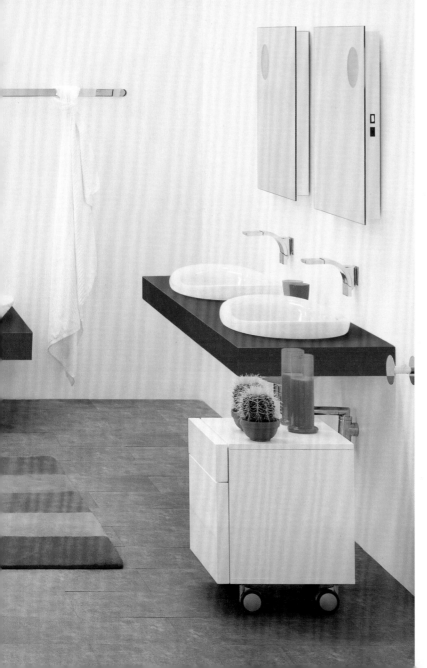

KALDEWEI
© Kaldewei

DORNBRACHT
© Dornbracht

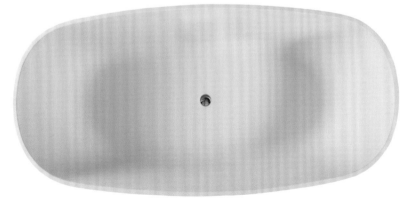

ANTONIO LUPI
© Antonio Lupi

KALDEWEI
© Kaldewei

KALDEWEI
© Kaldewei

BETTE
© Bette

DEVON & DEVON
© Devon & Devon

KALDEWEI
© Kaldewei

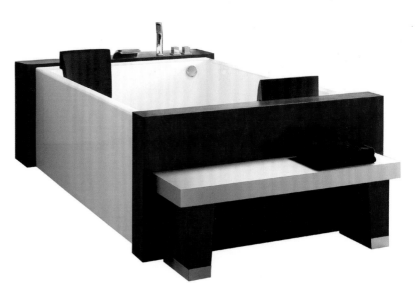

ANTONIO LUPI
© Antonio Lupi

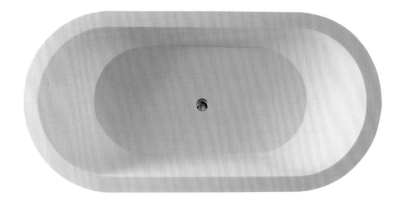

ANTONIO LUPI
© Antonio Lupi

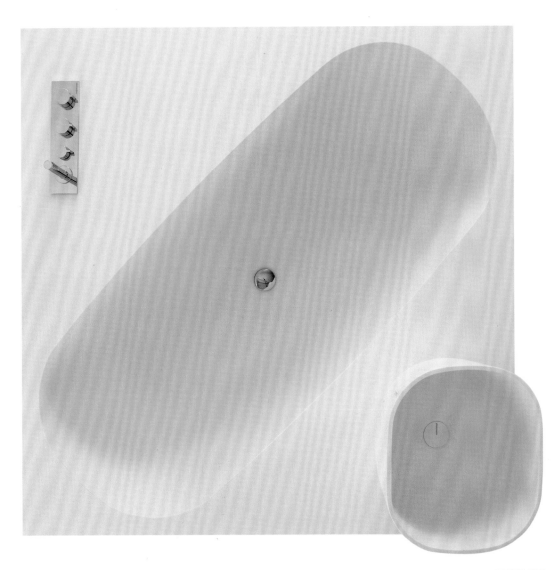

ANTONIO LUPI
© Antonio Lupi

BETTE
© Bette

DEVON & DEVON
Celine
© Devon & Devon

BETTE
© Bette

BETTE
© Bette

BETTE
© Bette

DEVON & DEVON
Elite
© Devon & Devon

DEVON & DEVON
Vasca Regina
© Devon & Devon

DEVON & DEVON
Vasca Regina
© Devon & Devon

DEVON & DEVON
Camelot
© Devon & Devon

REXA DESIGN
© Rexa Design

ALAPE
Be Yourself
© Alape

SPAS
SPAS
SPA
SPA
SPAS
SPA
SPA

Having a water massage tub at home is still synonymous with luxury and status, even though it is a good choice for anyone wanting to pamper themselves.

Avoir un spa chez soi est synonyme de luxe , bien que ce soit aussi une option envisageable pour ceux qui veulent prendre soin de leur corps et de leur esprit.

Eine Hydromassage zu Hause zu haben ist immer noch ein Sinnbild für Luxus und Status und dient der äußeren und inneren Pflege gleichermaßen.

Een hydromassage in huis staat nog altijd symbool voor luxe en status. Maar het is een goede optie voor wie zich zowel van binnen als van buiten goed wil verzorgen.

Tener un hidromasaje en casa sigue siendo sinónimo de lujo y estatus, aunque es una opción para aquellos que quieren cuidarse.

Avere un idromassaggio a casa è tuttora sinonimo di lusso e status, ma potrebbe essere una possibilità per tutti quelli che vogliono prendersi cura di sé.

Ter uma hidromassagem em casa continua a ser sinónimo de luxo e estatuto, embora seja uma opção para aqueles que querem cuidar de si.

Att ha ett massagebadkar hemma är fortfarande en symbol för lyx och hög status. Det är ett val för dem som vill ta väl hand om både sitt yttre och sitt inre.

Massage tubs are the best spa choice at home. There are countless varieties in terms of size and features.

Les bassins d'hydromassage constituent la meilleure option de spa à domicile. Ils se déclinent en un vaste choix de tailles et d'options.

Die Badewannen mit Hydromassage sind die beste Spa-Option. Es gibt sie in diversen Größen und Leistungsklassen.

Badkuipen met hydromassage zijn het beste alternatief als je thuis een spa wilt creëren. Er is een enorme keuze in grootte en vermogen.

Las bañeras de hidromasaje se presentan como la mejor opción del spa en casa. Existen innumerables modelos según el tamaño y las prestaciones.

Le vasche da bagno con idromassaggio rappresentano la migliore scelta per avere una spa a casa. Esiste una vasta gamma di vasche che va in base alle dimensioni e alle prestazioni.

As banheiras de hidromassagem apresentam-se como a melhor opção do spa em casa. Existem inúmeros modelos segundo o tamanho e os desempenhos.

Badkar med vattenmassage brukar presenteras som det bästa valet för ett hemmaspa. Det finns många att välja på, med olika storlek och prestanda.

Speak with a professional before beginning construction for advice on placing the spa tub and making the most of the space.

Consultez un spécialiste avant de commencer les travaux car il vous conseillera sur le meilleur endroit où placer le spa, ainsi que sur la façon de bien exploiter l'espace dont vous disposez.

Suchen Sie den Rat eines Fachmanns auf, bevor Sie die Bauarbeiten ausführen, da dieser weiß, welcher Ort sich am besten eignet, um das Spa zu platzieren und wie man den Raum am besten nutzt.

Laat je voor elke verbouwing altijd adviseren door een professional. Hij of zij kan meedenken over de beste plaats voor de spa, zodat de ruimte goed wordt gebruikt.

Acude a un profesional para que te aconseje sobre el mejor lugar para colocar el spa y cómo aprovechar bien el espacio.

Rivolgetevi ad un professionista: vi consiglierà il posto migliore per collocare la spa e sfruttare al meglio lo spazio.

Consulte um profissional pois poderá aconselhá-lo sobre o melhor lugar para colocar o spa e aproveitar bem o espaço.

Ta hjälp av ett proffs innan du gör någon form av renovering eftersom han eller hon kan ge råd om den bästa placeringen för ett spa, så att utrymmet utnyttjas på bästa sätt.

A good water massage should guarantee therapeutic results and offer the benefits of muscle massage to activate organ functions.

Un bon hydromassage doit apporter des résultats thérapeutiques et offrir les bienfaits d'un massage musculaire afin d'activer les processus organiques.

Eine gute Hydromassage garantiert gute therapeutische Ergebnisse und bietet den Vorteil der Muskelmassage, um die organischen Prozesse zu aktivieren.

Een goede hydromassage heeft gegarandeerd therapeutische effecten. Zo worden met de massage van de spieren de processen van de organen gestimuleerd.

El hidromasaje garantiza resultados terapéuticos y mediante el masaje muscular activa los procesos orgánicos.

Un buon idromassaggio deve garantire risultati terapeutici e dona il beneficio del massaggio muscolare per attivare i processi organici.

A hidromassagem garante resultados terapêuticos a partir da massagem muscular que ativa os processos orgânicos.

Ett bra massagebadkar ska garantera terapeutiska resultat och erbjuda muskelmassage som aktiverar organiska processer.

Some models come with water-based therapies like ozone therapy, colour therapy, magnet therapy and ionisation.

Certains modèles proposent des thérapies dans l'eau comme l'ozonothérapie, la chromothérapie, la magnétothérapie ou encore l'ionisation.

Einige Modelle beinhalten Wassertherapien, wie zum Beispiel die Ozontherapie, die Chromtherapie, die Magnettherapie oder die Ionisierung.

Sommige modellen worden geleverd met speciale waterbehandelingen bijvoorbeeld ozontherapie, chromotherapie, magneettherapie of ionisatietherapie.

Algunos modelos incorporan terapias en el agua como la ozonoterapia, la cromoterapia, la magnetoterapia o la ionización.

Alcuni modelli includono terapie nell'acqua come l'ozonoterapia, la cromoterapia, la magnetoterapia o la ionizzazione.

Alguns modelos incluem terapias na água como a ozonoterapia, a cromoterapia, a magnetoterapia ou a ionização.

Vissa modeller erbjuder vattenbehandlingar som ozonbehandling, krombehandling, magnetbehandling eller jonisering.

Bear in mind the sturdiness and characteristics of the chosen material. Highly resistant shells are recommended.

Tenez compte de la résistance et du comportement du matériau choisi. Il est recommandé d'opter pour un bassin haute résistance.

Beachten Sie die Widerstandskraft und das Verhalten des ausgewählten Materials. Es werden freitragende, widerstandsfähige Verkleidungen empfohlen.

Houd rekening met de degelijkheid van het materiaal dat je kiest en hoe het zich gedraagt. Kies bij voorkeur een zeer sterke zelfdragende constructie.

Ten en cuenta la resistencia y el comportamiento del material escogido. Se recomiendan los cascos de alta resistencia.

Prendete in considerazione la resistenza e il comportamento del materiale scelto. Si raccomanda l'uso di coperture ad alta resistenza.

Tenha em conta a resistência e o comportamento do material escolhido. São recomendados os cascos de alta resistência.

Tänk på tåligheten och underhållet hos det material som du väljer. Ytskikt med hög tålighet och självrengöring rekommenderas.

The depth of the massage is measured by the power of the motor, which ensures the massage quality.

La profondeur du massage sera fonction de la puissance du moteur, qui garantit la qualité du massage.

Die Tiefe der Massage wird durch die Motorpotenz gemessen, was die Qualität der Massage garantiert.

De diepte van de massage wordt gemeten aan de hand van het vermogen van de motor. Deze bepaalt de kwaliteit van de massage.

La profundidad del masaje se mide por la potencia del motor, que garantiza su calidad.

La profondità del massaggio è misurata in base alla potenza del motore che garantisce la qualità del massaggio.

A profundidade da massagem mede-se pela potência do motor, que garante a qualidade da massagem.

Massagens grundlighet mäts genom motorns prestanda, och ger garanti för kvaliteten på massagen.

The systems should ensure complete water drainage, along with the cleaning and disinfection of fungi and bacteria.

Les systèmes doivent assurer une évacuation totale de l'eau, ainsi que le nettoyage et la désinfection des champignons et des bactéries.

Die Systeme müssen das vollständige Abfließen des Wassers sowie die Reinigung und Desinfektion von Pilzen und Bakterien sicher stellen.

Voor alle systemen geldt dat al het water eruit weg moet kunnen lopen en dat ze goed schoon gehouden en ontsmet moeten kunnen worden, zodat er geen schimmels en bacteriën in ontstaan.

Los sistemas deben asegurar el total escurrimiento del agua y la limpieza y desinfección de hongos y bacterias.

I sistemi devono assicurare lo scorrimento totale dell'acqua, la pulizia e la disinfezione da funghi e batteri.

Os sistemas devem assegurar o total escorrimento da água e a limpeza e desinfeção de fungos e bactérias.

Systemet ska säkerställa att vattnet töms fullständigt och att det är möjligt att rengöra och desinficera helt för att avlägsna svampar och bakterier.

JACUZZI®
© Jacuzzi®

ARCHITECTS EAT
© Shania Shegedyn

ARCHITECTS EAT
© Shania Shegedyn

OCTAVIO MESTRE
© Jordi Miralles

OCTAVIO MESTRE
© Jordi Miralles

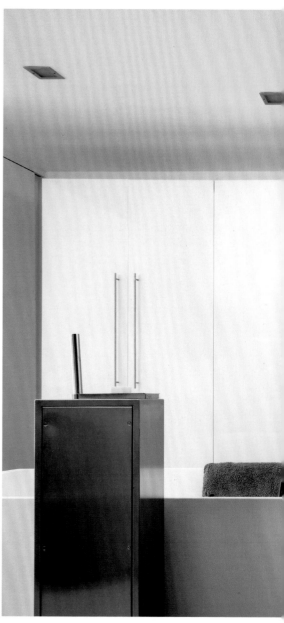

NICO HEYSSE
© Laurent Brandajs

JACUZZI®
© Jacuzzi®

© Jordi Miralles

© Jordi Miralles

© José Luis Hausmann

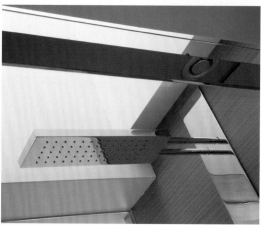

JACUZZI®
© Jacuzzi®

EX-IT ARCHITECTURE
© Courtesy of Ex-it Architecture

FURNITURE
MEUBLES
MÖBEL
MEUBILAIR
MOBILIARIO
ARREDAMENTO
MOBILIÁRIO
INREDNING

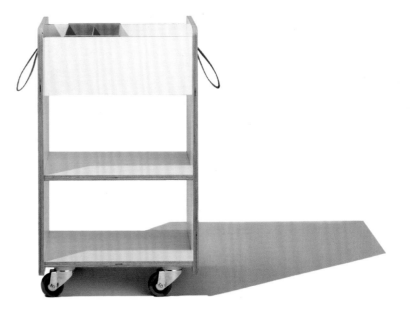

When selecting bathroom furniture, carefully analyse the size of the space available and how it will be used.

Au moment de choisir les meubles de votre salle de bains, vous devez évaluer l'espace dont vous disposez et bien déterminer la fonction de chacun d'entre eux.

Bei der Wahl des Badezimmermöbels sollte man den Raum und die Funktion berücksichtigen.

Ga bij het maken van een keuze voor het badkamermeubilair uit van de grootte van de beschikbare ruimte en bedenk waar het meubilair voor gebruikt gaat worden.

A la hora de elegir los muebles del baño, debes analizar bien las dimensiones del espacio disponible y la función que van a desempeñar.

Nel momento della scelta dei mobili del bagno, dovrete analizzare bene le dimensioni dello spazio disponibile e la funzione che dovranno svolgere.

Na altura de escolher os móveis da casa de banho, deve analisar bem o tamanho do espaço disponível e a função que vão desempenhar.

När man väljer inredning till badrummet ska man noga överväga storleken på utrymmet och den funktion som det ska fylla.

For smaller bathrooms, try to find furniture that enhances visual breadth with designs that integrate essential features in a single piece.

Si votre salle de bains est petite, privilégiez des meubles qui vous aident à créer une sensation d'espace.

Wenn man nur ein kleines Bad hat, muss man Möbel aussuchen, die größer wirken.

Heb je een kleine badkamer, zoek dan naar meubels waarmee de ruimte groter lijkt.

Si tienes un baño pequeño hay que buscar muebles que te ayuden a ganar amplitud visual.

Se avete un bagno piccolo, occorre cercare mobili che aiutino a guadagnare ampiezza visiva.

Se dispuser de uma casa de banho pequena, tem de procurar os móveis que o ajudem a ganhar amplitude visual.

Har man ett litet badkar gäller det att hitta inredning som ökar intrycket av rymlighet.

Plants are a good idea since they purify the air. If plants are not enough, you can also use a dehumidifier.

Il est recommandé d'avoir des plantes dans votre salle de bains car elles purifient l'air. Si les plantes ne suffisent pas, vous pouvez réduire l'humidité dans la pièce grâce à une ventilation.

Auch sind luftreinigende Pflanzen empfehlenswert. Zusätzlich kann ein Entfeuchter in Form eines Ventilators dienen.

De aanwezigheid van planten kan zorgen voor luchtzuivering. Als dit niet voldoende werkt, dan kan ook een ontvochtiger (bijvoorbeeld een ventilator) worden gebruikt.

La presencia de plantas es aconsejable ya que purifican el aire. Si las plantas no son suficientes se puede usar un deshumidificador.

È consigliabile la presenza di piante poiché purificano l'aria. Se le piante non sono sufficienti, è possibile utilizzare un deumidificatore.

A presença de plantas é aconselhável uma vez que purificam o ar. Se as plantas não forem suficientes, pode-se usar um desumidificador.

Det är bra att ha krukväxter eftersom de renar luften. Om det inte räcker kan man använda en luftavfuktare som komplement till ventilationen.

Modular furniture promotes space saving, the use of fewer resources and neater surfaces.

L'utilisation d'un mobilier modulable permet de gagner de l'espace, de réduire l'emploi de ressources et de bénéficier de surfaces dégagées.

Der Gebrauch von Modulmöbeln sorgt für mehr Platz. Sie sind preisgünstig und man erfreut sich an sauberen Oberflächen.

Met het gebruik van wandmeubels bespaar je ruimte en geld. Bovendien worden ze minder snel vuil.

El uso de mobiliario modular permite ahorrar espacio, reducir el empleo de recursos y disfrutar de superficies limpias.

L'uso di mobili modulari consente di risparmiare spazio, ridurre l'impiego di risorse e sfruttare superfici pulite.

O uso de mobiliário modular permite poupar espaço, reduzir o emprego de recursos e desfrutar de superfícies limpas.

Modulinredning hjälper dig att spara utrymme, utnyttja slantarna på bästa sätt och få ytor som lätt hålls rena.

Some companies offer stone designs in simple, natural shapes. This is an extremely elegant return to our roots.

Certaines entreprises proposent des meubles en pierre, au design simple et naturel. C'est un retour aux sources très élégant.

Einige Firmen präsentieren Designs aus Stein in einfachen und natürlichen Formen. Ganz elegant kehrt man dadurch zurück zu den Ursprüngen.

Sommige bedrijven leveren stenen ontwerpen in eenvoudige en natuurlijke vormen. Zo creëer je met smaak een back to basics.

Algunas firmas presentan diseños de piedra de formas simples y naturales. Es un retorno a los orígenes con mucha elegancia.

Alcune marche presentano modelli di pietra aventi forme semplici e naturali. Si tratta di un ritorno alle origini con grande eleganza.

Algumas empresas oferecem modelos de pedra de formas simples e naturais. É um regresso às origens com muita elegância.

Vissa firmor erbjuder design av sten i enkel och naturlig form. Det är en återkoppling till naturen med mycket elegans.

For those who are seeking a more luxurious aesthetic, some bathrooms are equipped with ceramic materials crafted using clean technology criteria.

Pour ceux qui recherchent une esthétique plus luxueuse, il existe des salles de bains équipées de matériaux céramiques, fabriqués par le biais de technologies propres.

Für Liebhaber luxuriöserer Ästhetik gibt es Bäder, die mit Materialien aus Keramik ausgestattet sind, welche nach den Kriterien sauberer Technologien gefertigt wurden.

Wie van meer luxe houdt, kan kiezen voor een badkamer met veel keramisch materiaal, dat conform schone technologische normen is gefabriceerd.

Para los que requieran una estética lujosa, existen baños equipados con materiales fabricados según criterios de tecnologías limpias.

Per quanti ricerchino un'estetica più lussuosa esistono bagni attrezzati con materiali di ceramica, fabbricati secondo criteri di tecnologie pulite.

Para os que exigem uma estética mais luxuosa, existem casas de banho equipadas com materiais cerâmicos, fabricados segundo critérios de tecnologias limpas.

För dem som vill ha en lyxigare stil finns det badkar av keramik som tillverkas enligt miljövänliga kriterier.

Simple lines are always preferable in a bathroom. Select furniture made from natural materials like teak.

Pour la salle de bains, il est préférable d'opter pour des lignes simples. Choisissez des meubles en matériaux naturels comme le teck.

Im Bad sind immer einfache Linien vorzuziehen. Suchen Sie Möbel aus natürlichen Materialien aus, wie zum Beispiel aus Teak.

Het geniet in badkamers altijd de voorkeur eenvoudige lijnen te gebruiken. Kies bijvoorbeeld voor meubels van natuurlijk materiaal, zoals teakhout.

Las líneas simples en el baño son siempre preferibles. Elige muebles de materiales naturales como la teca.

Nel bagno sono sempre preferibili le linee semplici. Scegliete mobili in materiali naturali come il tek.

As linhas simples na casa de banho são sempre preferíveis. Escolha móveis de materiais naturais como a teca.

Enkla linjer i badrummet är alltid att föredra. Välj inredning av naturmaterial, som teak.

Choose accent furniture with wheels, shelves, hanging cabinets and extendible hangers. Select in accordance with visual preference

Choisissez des meubles d'appoint sur roues, des étagères et armoires suspendues ainsi que des patères en fonction de l'impact visuel que vous recherchez.

Man sollte zusätzliche Möbelstücke auswählen, die Rollen haben sowie Regale, Hängeschränke und leichte Bügel. Wichtig ist dabei natürlich auch die Optik

Kies verrijdbare bijzetmeubels en rekken, kasten en haakjes die aan de muur zijn bevestigd. Let daarbij op hoeveel ruimte ze innemen.

Elige muebles auxiliares con ruedas, estanterías, armarios colgados y perchas voladas en función del peso visual.

Scegliete mobili, accessori con rotelle, scaffali, armadi appesi e attaccapanni sporgenti in funzione del peso visivo che volete conferirgli.

Escolha móveis auxiliares com rodas, estantes, armários suspensos e cabides pequenos. Escolha-os em função do peso visual que lhes quiser atribuir.

Välj möbler som underlättar, med hjul, hyllor, väggmonterad förvaring och vägghängda krokar. Välj dem med tanke på funktion och visuellt intryck.

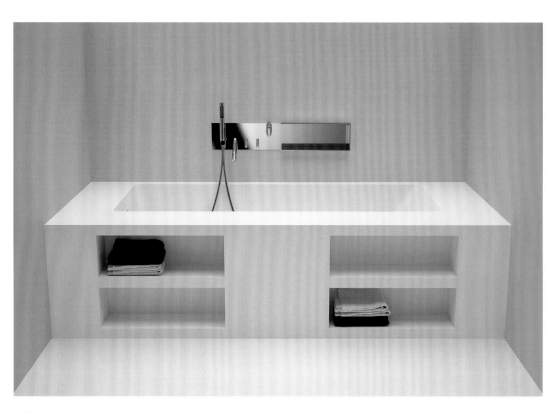

AGAPE
© Agape

SONIA
© Sonia

DURAVIT
© Duravit

© José Luis Hausmann

KEUCO
© Keuco

KALDEWEI

© Kaldewei

AGAPE

DECOLAV
© Decolav

BURGBAD
© Burgbad

AXIA
© Axia

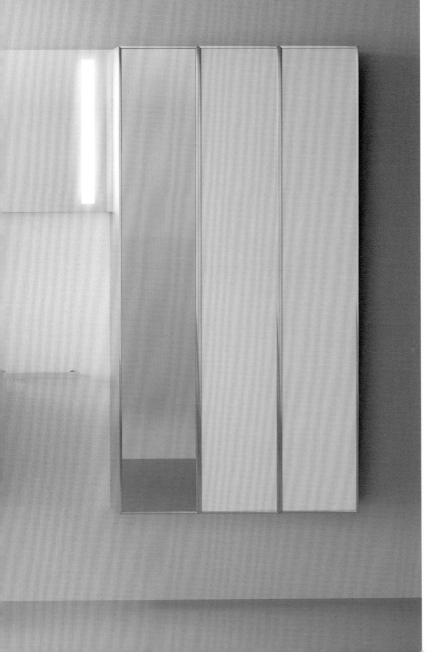

BURGBAD
© Burgbad

HARDY INSIDE
© Hardy Inside

DURAVIT
© Duravit

COGLIATI
© Cogliati

HABITAT
© Habitat

KOHLER
© Kohler

FORMER
© Former

DURAVIT
© Duravit

POM D'OR
© Pom d'Or

DECOLAV
© Decolav

HARDY INSIDE
© Hardy Inside

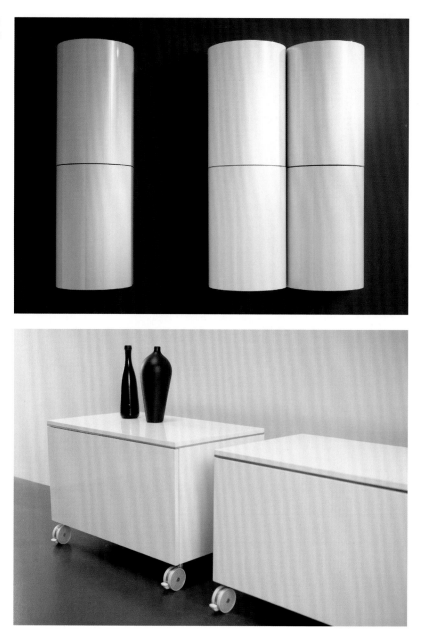

LAUFEN
Mimo
© Laufen

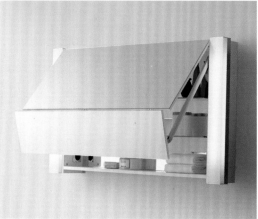

BURGBAD
© Burgbad

INBANI

© Inbani

LAUFEN
Mimo
© Laufen

LAUFEN
Mimo
© Laufen

LAUFEN
Mimo
© Laufen

KOHLER
© Kohler

STONE FOREST
Siena Line
© Stone Forest

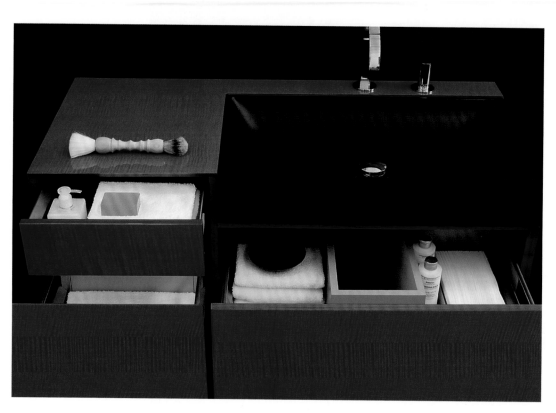

REGIA
© Regia

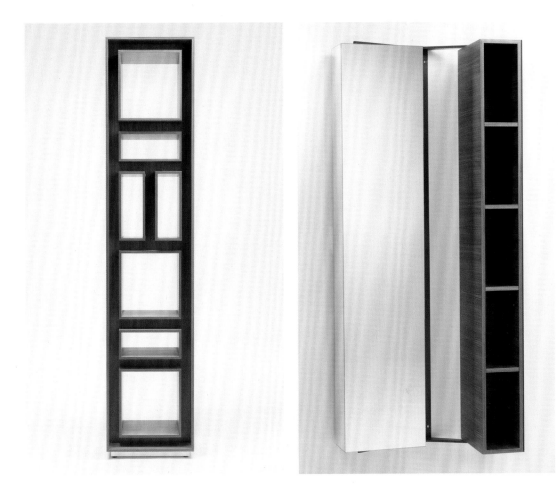

POM D'OR
© Pom d'Or

POM D'OR
© Pom d'Or

ACCESSORIES

ACCESSOIRES

ZUBEHÖR

ACCESSOIRES

ACCESORIOS

ACCESSORI

ACESSÓRIOS

TILLBEHÖR

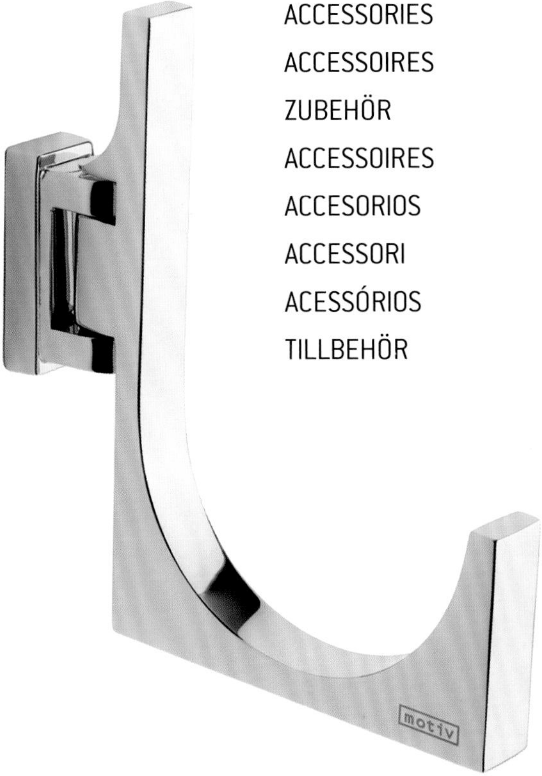

Accessories should be selected according to the bathroom design: you can choose from traditional to country, minimalist or total luxury.

Choisissez les accessoires en fonction du style de votre salle de bains. Vous pouvez choisir un style traditionnel, rustique, minimaliste ou encore luxueux.

Das funktionale Zubehör wird nach dem Stil des Bads ausgewählt: man kann sich für einen traditionellen Stil, einen ländlichen, minimalistischen oder einfach luxuriösen Stil entscheiden.

Kies accessoires die bij de stijl van de badkamer passen. Je kunt bijvoorbeeld kiezen voor klassiek, rustiek, minimalistisch of luxe.

Los accesorios se escogerán en función del estilo del baño: puedes optar por un estilo tradicional, campestre, minimalista o lujoso.

Scegliete gli accessori in funzione dello stile del bagno: potete optare per uno stile tradizionale, campestre, minimalista o lussuoso.

Escolhem-se os acessórios em função do estilo da casa de banho: é possível optar por um estilo tradicional, campestre, minimalista ou luxuoso.

Man ska välja tillbehör som passar stilen på badrummet: man kan välja en traditionell, lantlig, minimalistisk eller lyxig stil.

To achieve total harmony, a good solution is to complement the accessories to the taps that are already installed.

Afin d'obtenir une harmonie parfaite, une bonne solution consiste à choisir les accessoires en fonction des robinets déjà en place.

Um insgesamt Harmonie zu erzeugen, ist es empfehlenswert, das Zubehör insgesamt in Übereinstimmung mit den installierten Armaturen abzustimmen.

Om een harmonieus geheel te creëren, is het een goed idee om de accessoires te kiezen in de stijl van het reeds geïnstalleerde kraanwerk.

Para conseguir la total armonía, una buena solución es elegir accesorios acordes con la grifería previamente instalada.

Per raggiungere l'armonia totale, una buona soluzione è scegliere gli accessori abbinati con le rubinetterie installate in precedenza.

Para conseguir a total harmonia, uma boa solução é escolher os acessórios de acordo com as torneiras previamente instaladas.

För att uppnå fullständig harmoni är det en bra lösning att välja tillbehör som matchar den blandare som monterats.

Their positioning also plays a key role in the entirety. If the pieces to be installed are poorly placed, there may be no solution.

Une erreur d'appréciation ne pourra pas toujours être corrigée, par exemple dans le cas où l'accessoire est fixé.

Der Standort spielt beim Gesamtbild ebenfalls eine große Rolle. Ist er nicht gut gewählt, können spätere Installationen schwierig werden.

De plaatsing van de accessoires speelt een belangrijke rol in het totaalbeeld. Denk van tevoren goed na waar en hoe ze geplaatst moeten worden.

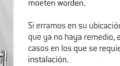

Si erramos en su ubicación puede que ya no haya remedio, en los casos en los que se requiere una instalación.

Se sbagliamo a disporli, nei casi in cui è richiesta un'installazione, potrebbe non esserci più soluzione.

Se errarmos na localização, pode acontecer que já não haja solução, nos casos em que se exige uma instalação.

Placeringen spelar också stor roll för det sammanhängande intrycket. Om de installerade detaljerna placerats fel, kanske det inte finns någon lösning.

Towel racks, soap dispensers, hooks and other accessories are as important as surfaces and finishes.

Porte-serviettes, distributeurs de savon liquide et autres accessoires sont aussi importants que les surfaces et les finitions.

Handtuchhalter, Seifenspender, Haken und anderes Zubehör sind genauso wichtig wie die Oberflächen und die Endverarbeitung.

Handdoekrekken, zeepdispensers, kapstokken en andere accessoires zijn net zo belangrijk als de gehele afwerking.

Toalleros, dispensadores de jabón, colgadores y demás accesorios son tan importantes como las superficies y los acabados.

Portasciugamani, distributori di sapone, attaccapanni e altri accessori, sono ugualmente importanti quanto le superfici e le finiture.

Toalheiros, dispensadores de sabonete, cabides e outros acessórios, são tão importantes como as superfícies e os acabamentos.

Handdukshängare, tvålkoppar, krokar och andra tillbehör är lika viktiga som ytorna och inredningen.

Select a mirror equipped with an LED lighting system or halogen bulbs, which can be dimmed or brightened.

Choisissez un miroir comprenant un système d'éclairage LED ou un système halogène gradateur de lumière.

Wählen Sie einen Spiegel aus, der ein Beleuchtungssystem mit LED oder eine dimmbare Halogenbeleuchtung hat.

Kies voor een spiegel met LED verlichting of halogeenlampen die gedimd kunnen worden.

Elige un espejo que incorpore sistemas de iluminación con led o iluminación alógena que pueda graduarse.

Scegliete uno specchio che includa sistemi d'illuminazione LED, o illuminazione alogena regolabile.

Escolha um espelho que inclua sistemas de iluminação com LED, ou iluminação de halogéneo que seja possível graduar.

Välj en spegel som innehåller LED-belysning eller halogenbelysning med anpassningsbar styrka.

Choose mirrors that allow personal effects to be stored behind them. Some are also equipped with a heating system to prevent them from steaming up after a shower.

Optez pour des miroirs avec armoire de rangement. Certaines comportent même un élément chauffant afin d'éviter que le miroir soit embué.

Wählen Sie Spiegel aus, hinter denen man Sachen verstauen kann. Einige bieten sogar ein Heizsystem an, damit der Spiegel beim Duschen nicht beschlägt.

Spiegels met daarachter ruimte om allerlei zaken op te bergen zijn erg handig. Soms is er een warmtesysteem ingebouwd waardoor er geen condens neerslaat na het douchen.

Opta por espejos que permitan almacenar los enseres en la parte posterior. Algunos incorporan un sistema de calor para evitar que se empañen.

Optate per specchi che consentano di custodire oggetti. Alcuni sono addirittura dotati di un sistema di riscaldamento che ne evita l'appannamento.

Opte por espelhos que permitam armazenar os utensílios. Alguns incluem um sistema de calor para evitar que embaciem.

Välj gärna en spegel som man kan ställa in saker i. Vissa har till och med uppvärmning för att de inte ska imma igen när man duschar.

Selecting materials that
complement each other will also
help to achieve a given decor.

Optez pour des matériaux que
vous pouvez combiner, afin
d'obtenir un style décoratif défini.

Wählen Sie Materialien aus, die
gut miteinander kombiniert
werden können, da dadurch ein
festgelegter, dekorativer Stil
erreicht wird.

Kies voor materialen die goed met
elkaar te combineren zijn, zodat je
een bepaalde decoratiestijl kunt
creëren.

Elige materiales que combinen
entre sí ya que te ayudarán a
conseguir un estilo decorativo
determinado.

Scegliete materiali che si
combinino fra loro poiché vi
aiuteranno ad ottenere un
determinato stile decorativo.

Escolha materiais que combinem
entre si, pois irão ajudá-lo a
conseguir um estilo decorativo
determinado.

Välj material som passar bra ihop
eftersom det hjälper dig att uppnå
en dekorativ designstil.

There are finishes on the market
that use recycled materials that
are glued using polyurethane
cord.

Il existe sur le marché des
revêtements à base de matériaux
recyclés, assemblés par le biais
de polyuréthanne.

Auf dem Markt gibt es
Verkleidungen aus recyceltem
Material, die ein Haltesystem
mit Schnüren aus Polyurethan
verwenden.

Er is bijvoorbeeld gerecycled
bekledingsmateriaal te koop
dat wordt bevestigd met
polyurethaanlijm.

Existen revestimientos en
el mercado con materiales
reciclados que utilizan un
sistema de pegado con cordón de
poliuretano.

Esistono sul mercato dei
rivestimenti con materiali riciclati
che utilizzano un sistema
d'incollaggio con cordone adesivo
in poliuretano.

Existem revestimentos no
mercado com materiais reciclados
que utilizam um sistema
de colagem com cordão de
poliuretano.

Det finns ytmaterial på
marknaden som är gjorda av
återvunnet material med ett
bindningssystem av polyuretan.

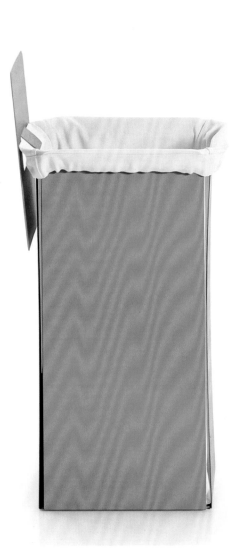

LINEA BETA
© Linea Beta

LINEA BETA
© Linea Beta

LINEA BETA
© Linea Beta

DECOR WALTHER
© Decor Walther

DECOR WALTHER
© Decor Walther

POM D'OR
© Pom d'Or

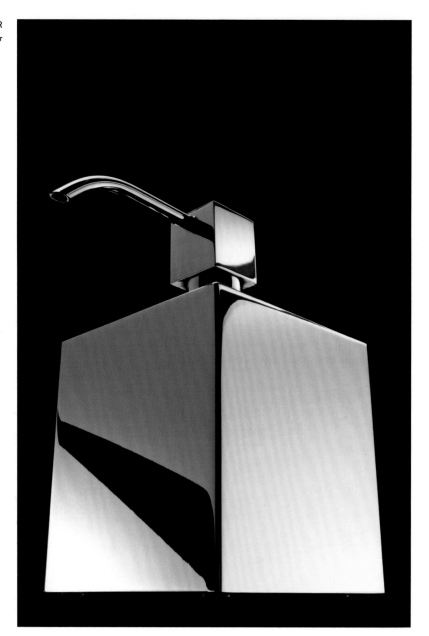

DECOR WALTHER
© Decor Walther

DECOR WALTHER
© Decor Walther

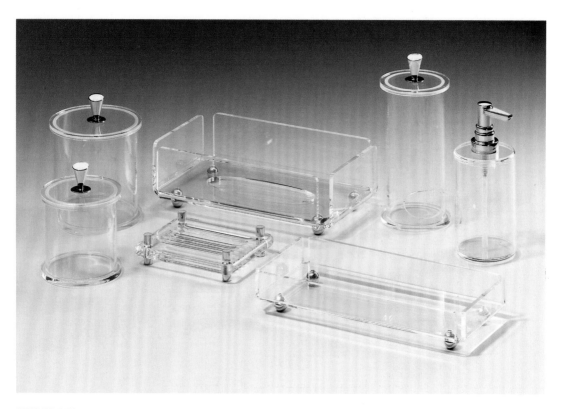

DECOR WALTHER
© Decor Walther

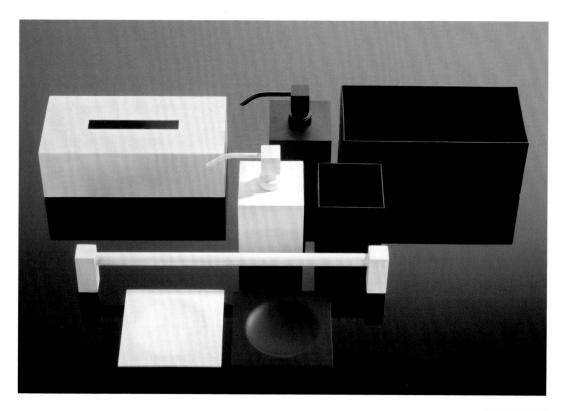

DECOR WALTHER
© Decor Walther

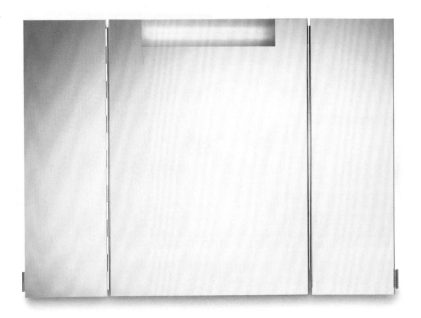

DECOR WALTHER
© Decor Walther

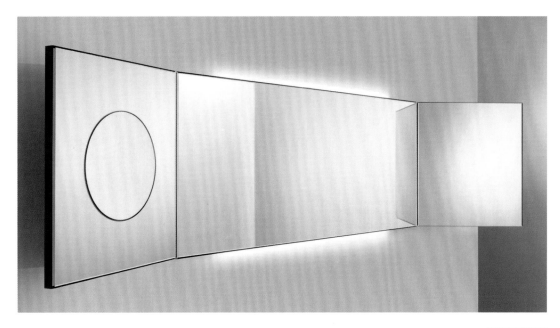

DECOR WALTHER
© Decor Walther

DECOR WALTHER
© Decor Walther

DECOR WALTHER
© Decor Walther

DECOR WALTHER
© Decor Walther

DECOR WALTHER
© Decor Walther

DECOR WALTHER
© Decor Walther

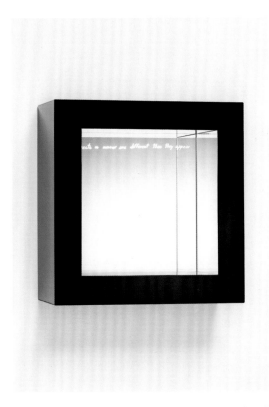

GLAS ITALIA
© Glas Italia

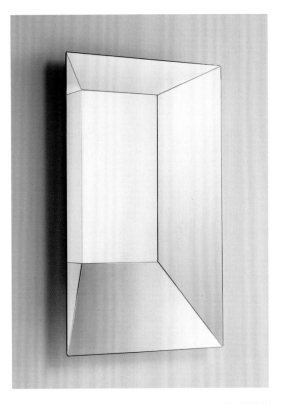

GLAS ITALIA
© Glas Italia

REGIA
© Regia

OLYMPIA CERAMICA
Ukiyo-E
© Olympia Ceramica

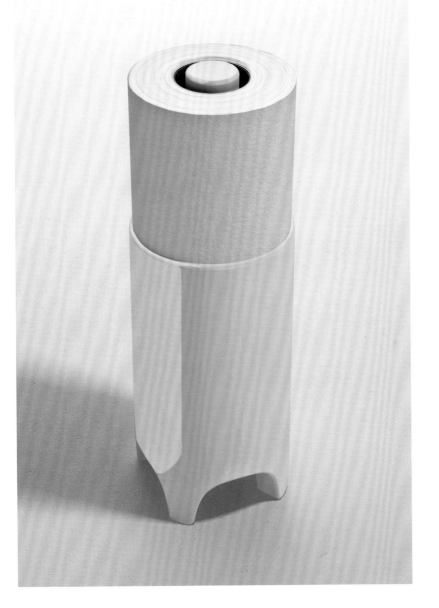

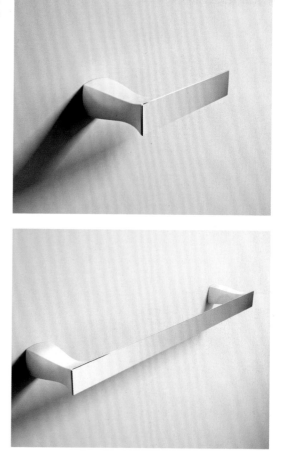

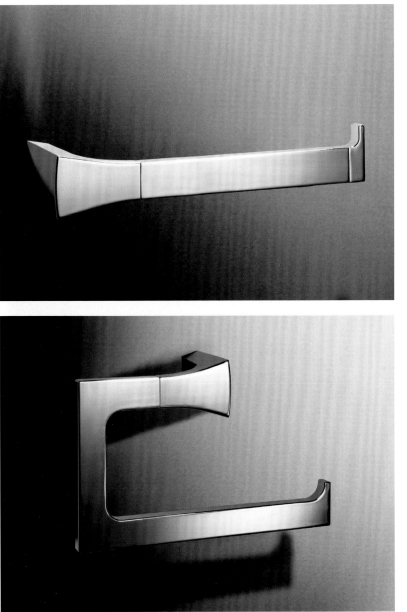

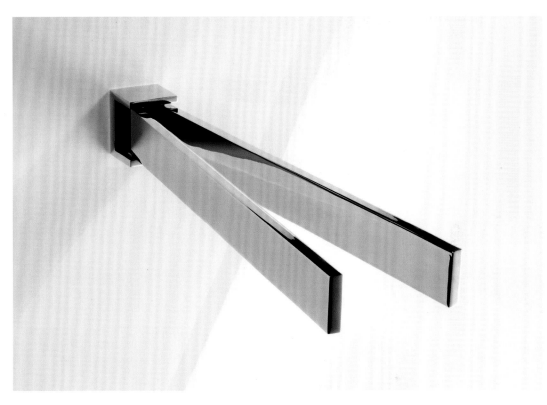

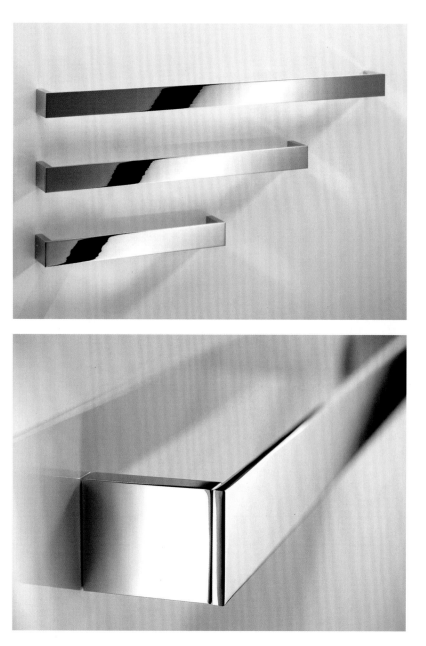

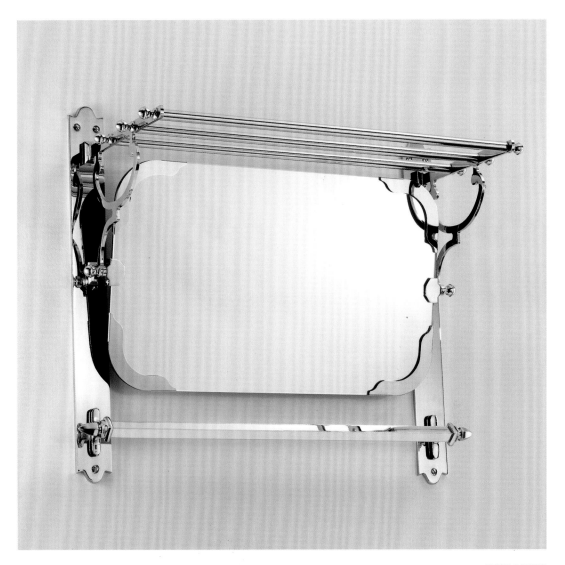

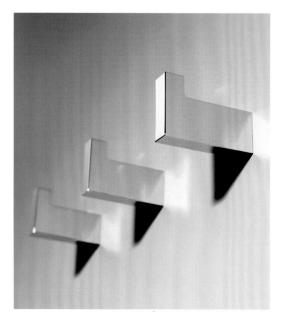

POM D'OR
© Pom d'Or

REGIA
© Regia

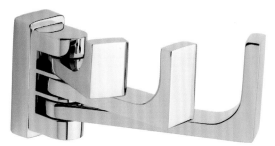

BRASSTECH
© Brasstech

INDA
© Inda

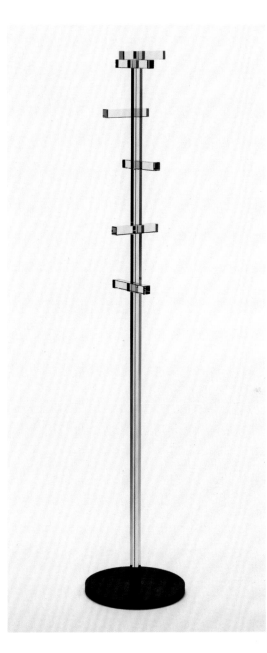

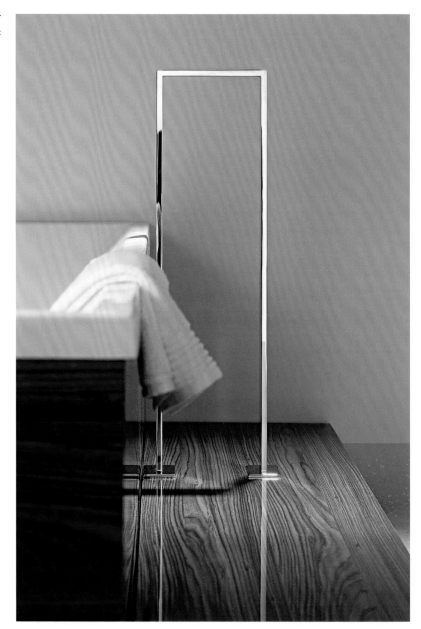

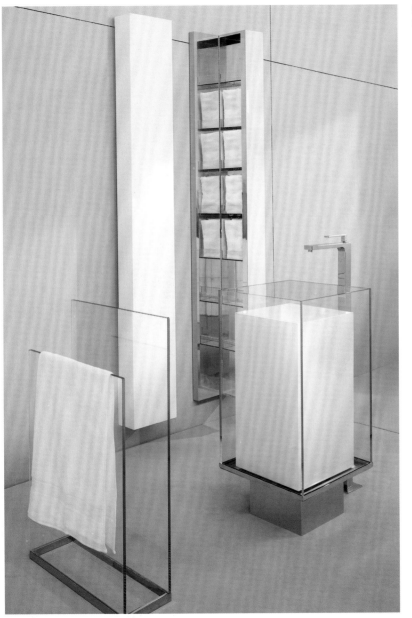

DIRECTORY

Agape
www.agapedesign.it

ALAPE
www.alape.com

Alessi
www.alessi.com

Althea Ceramica
www.altheaceramica.it

Antonio Lupi
www.antoniolupi.it

Aquatic Industries
www.aquaticwhirlpools.com

Artceram
www.artceram.it

Artquitects Eat
www.eatas.com.au

Artquitect
www.artquitect.net

Axia
www.axiabath.com

Axor ffl Hansgrohe International
www.axor-design.com

Bette
www.bette.de

Bisazza
www.bisazza.com

Bluform
www.bluform.eu

Brasstech
www.brasstech.com

Boffi
www.boffi.com

Burgbad
www.burgbad.com

Cesana
www.cesana.it

Ceramica Flaminia
www.ceramicaflaminia.it

Cifial
www.cifial.pt

Cogliati
www.cogliati-cogliati.it

Decolav
www.decolav.com

Decor Walther
www.decor-walther.de

Devon & Devon
www.devon-devon.com

Duravit
www.duravit.es

Dornbracht
www.dornbracht.com

Envirolet® by Sancor Industries Ltd.
www.sancorindustries.com

EX-IT Architecture
www.ex-it.be

Filip Deslee
www.loft4c.be

Former
www.former.com

Gamadecor
www.gama-decor.com

Gessi
www.gessi.com

Glas Italia
www.glasitalia.com

Graff Faucets
www.graff-faucets.com

Grup Gamma
www.gamma.es

Habitat
www.habitat.net

Hardy Inside
www.hardyinside.com

IB Rubinetterie
www.ibrubinetterie.it

Ikea
www.ikea.com

Inbani
www.inbani.com

Inda
www.inda.net

Ivano Redaelli
www.ivanoredaelli.it

Jaclo
www.jaclo.com

Julien
www.julien.ca

Jacuzzi®
http://es.jacuzzi.eu

Kaldewei
www.kaldewei.es

Kanera
www.kanera.de

Keuco
www.keuco.de

Kohler
www.us.kohler.com

KWC
www.kwc.ch

Landau + Kindelbacher
www.landaukindelbacher.de

Laufen
www.laufen.com

Linea Beta
www.lineabeta.it

Long Tsai Corporation
www.longtsai.com

Newform
www.newform.it

Nico Heysse
nicoheysse@skynet.be

Octavio Mestre
www.octaviomestre.com

Olympia Ceramica
www.olympiaceramica.it

Pom d'Or
www.pomdor.com

Porcelanosa Grupo
www.porcelanosa.com

Regia
www.regia.it

Rexa Design
www.rexadesign.it

Richard Lampert
www.richard-lampert.de

Roca
www.roca.es

Sixx Design
www.sixxdesign.com

Smallbone of Devizes
www.smallbone.co.uk

Sonia
www.sonia-sa.com

Stone Forest
www.stoneforest.com

Vitra USA
www.vitra-usa.com

Villeroy & Boch
www.villeroy-boch.com

Vision Tiles & Bathroom
www.vision-direct.com.au

Yanko Design
www.yankodesign.com

Zazzeri
www.zazzeri.it

PHOTO CREDITS

P. 14: © Laufen
P. 42: © Decolav
P. 102: © Ceramica Flaminia
P. 142: © Jaclo
P. 176: © Ceramica Flaminia
P. 276: © Marcel Wanders for © Bisazza
P. 338: © Richard Lampert